Praise for
ONE SPIRIT MEDICINE

"One Spirit Medicine is the new manifesto for body
and soul. The wisdom of the ancients is being newly
discovered in the language of our biology. Alberto Villoldo
translates advances in the science of creating health and
integrates them with spiritual and life practices from shamanic
traditions—the one medicine we all need to reclaim body,
mind, and soul. There is no one better to guide us on
our journey toward living a light-filled, vibrant life."

— **Dr Mark Hyman**, author of #1 *New York Times* bestseller, *The
Blood Sugar Solution 10-Day Detox Diet,* and director of Cleveland
Clinic Center for Functional Medicine

"One Spirit Medicine offers an opportunity to
move beyond misperceived limitations and write new
empowering stories for our lives. With authority and eloquence,
Alberto Villoldo presents a paradigm-shattering synthesis
of wisdom traditions and modern science that enables the
reader to move from passive victim and become the master of
their fate. *One Spirit Medicine* is a powerful and wise prescription
for self-healing and an opportunity to
reclaim power over your health and your destiny."

— **Bruce H. Lipton PhD**, cell biologist, bestselling author of *The
Biology of Belief* and co-author of *Spontaneous Evolution*

"In *One Spirit Medicine* Alberto Villoldo artfully weds
traditional wisdom with leading-edge nutritional
science, delivering a program that pushes the
reset button, paving the way for health."

— **Dr David Perlmutter**, author of #1 *New York Times* bestseller,
*Grain Brain: The Surprising Truth About Wheat, Carbs and Sugar—
Your Brain's Silent Killers*

"Alberto Villoldo PhD does a brilliant job in carefully
demystifying age-old wisdom with practical cutting-edge science.
One Spirit Medicine is the big answer to our health-care problems
in the 21st century. This book will change your life."

— **Dr Joe Dispenza**, author of *New York Times* bestseller *You Are
the Placebo: Making Your Mind Matter* and *Breaking the Habit of
Being Yourself: How to Lose Your Mind and Create a New One*

"*One Spirit Medicine* is a powerful blend of spiritual philosophy and scientific principles woven into the perfection of a practical formula for everyday life! Easy-to-read, yet brimming with timeless wisdom, Alberto leads us on a journey of discovery that shatters common misconceptions about us, our relationship to our body, and the world. In doing so he reminds us that the key to our healing lies in our ability to embrace ourselves, and the world, as living, conscious, and connected. You'll want to keep this book at your fingertips."

— **Gregg Braden**, *New York Times* bestselling author of *The Divine Matrix* and *Deep Truth*

ONE SPIRIT MEDICINE

ALSO BY ALBERTO VILLOLDO PhD

POWER UP YOUR BRAIN: The Neuroscience of Enlightenment
(with Dr David Perlmutter)*

ILLUMINATION: The Shaman's Way of Healing*

COURAGEOUS DREAMING:
How Shamans Dream the World into Being*

THE FOUR INSIGHTS: Wisdom, Power,
and Grace of the Earthkeepers*

MENDING THE PAST AND HEALING
THE FUTURE WITH SOUL RETRIEVAL*

SHAMAN, HEALER, SAGE: How to Heal Yourself
and Others with the Energy Medicine of the Americas

THE REALMS OF HEALING (with Stanley Krippner)

DANCE OF THE FOUR WINDS: Secrets of the
Inca Medicine Wheel (with Erik Jendresen)

ISLAND OF THE SUN: Mastering the Inca Medicine Wheel
(with Erik Jendresen)

THE FOUR WINDS: A Shaman's Odyssey
into the Amazon (with Erik Jendresen)

HEALING STATES: A Journey into the World of Spiritual Healing
and Shamanism (with Stanley Krippner PhD)

*Available from Hay House
Please visit:

Hay House UK: www.hayhouse.co.uk
Hay House USA: www.hayhouse.com®
Hay House Australia: www.hayhouse.com.au
Hay House India: www.hayhouse.co.in

ONE SPIRIT MEDICINE

Ancient Ways to Ultimate Wellness

ALBERTO VILLOLDO

HAY HOUSE

Carlsbad, California • New York City • London • Sydney
Johannesburg • Vancouver • Hong Kong • New Delhi

First published and distributed in the United Kingdom by:
Hay House UK Ltd, Astley House, 33 Notting Hill Gate, London W11 3JQ
Tel: +44 (0)20 3675 2450; Fax: +44 (0)20 3675 2451; www.hayhouse.co.uk

Published and distributed in the United States of America by:
Hay House Inc., PO Box 5100, Carlsbad, CA 92018-5100
Tel: (1) 760 431 7695 or (800) 654 5126
Fax: (1) 760 431 6948 or (800) 650 5115; www.hayhouse.com

Published and distributed in Australia by:
Hay House Australia Ltd, 18/36 Ralph St, Alexandria NSW 2015
Tel: (61) 2 9669 4299; Fax: (61) 2 9669 4144; www.hayhouse.com.au

Published and distributed in the Republic of South Africa by:
Hay House SA (Pty) Ltd, PO Box 990, Witkoppen 2068
info@hayhouse.co.za

Published and distributed in India by:
Hay House Publishers India, Muskaan Complex, Plot No.3, B-2,
Vasant Kunj, New Delhi 110 070
Tel: (91) 11 4176 1620; Fax: (91) 11 4176 1630; www.hayhouse.co.in

Distributed in Canada by:
Raincoast Books, 2440 Viking Way, Richmond, B.C. V6V 1N2
Tel: (1) 604 448 7100; Fax: (1) 604 270 7161; www.raincoast.com

Copyright © 2015 by Alberto Villoldo

The moral rights of the author have been asserted.

The information given in this book should not be treated as a substitute for professional medical advice; always consult a medical practitioner. Any use of information in this book is at the reader's discretion and risk. Neither the author nor the publisher can be held responsible for any loss, claim or damage arising out of the use, or misuse, of the suggestions made, the failure to take medical advice or for any material on third party websites.

A catalogue record for this book is available from the British Library.

ISBN: 978-1-78180-480-3

Cover and book design: Tricia Breidenthal

Printed and bound in Great Britain by TJ International Ltd, Padstow, Cornwall

TO ELENA ARELLANO DE VILLOLDO
AND ELENA V. CARPENTER,
MOTHER AND SISTER, WITH LOVE

CONTENTS

INTRODUCTION

Everything was going well for me. Professionally I was at the top of my game, a best-selling author with 12 books to my credit, a researcher and medical anthropologist with a Ph.D. in psychology, a teacher and healer with a following worldwide. The Light Body School and the Four Winds Society that I founded had grown exponentially: more than 5,000 students had gone through our training in energy medicine or had accompanied me on journeys to the Amazon and the Andes. And those were just the accomplishments the public could see. Close to my heart were the many inner gifts I had received on my spiritual path, including the most precious gift of all, a beloved partner who walks the path beside me.

Just when it looked as if life couldn't get any better, I was stopped in my tracks. Suddenly I was in a fight for survival that called on everything I'd learned in 30 years of studying with some of the world's most gifted healers. You see, I am also a shaman, trained in the ancient healing ways of indigenous peoples in the jungles and mountains of South America, the Caribbean, and Asia.

Clearly the Amazon rain forest is not the Beverly Hilton, so when I tell people what I do, they often say, "Are you nuts?" I understand their concern. The way of the shaman is not for everyone. The training is rigorous and demanding, and it extracted a heavy price.

I was in Mexico, a keynote speaker at a conference on shamanism, when without warning, I found I couldn't walk a hundred feet without collapsing in exhaustion. Friends chalked it up to my crazy travel schedule, but I knew something was terribly wrong.

A few days before the trip I had received a head-to-toe check-up, complete with a battery of tests, from medical specialists in Miami. When I called my doctors from Mexico, the news was not good. Apparently, during my years of research in Indonesia, Africa, and South America I had picked up a long list of nasty microorganisms, including five different kinds of hepatitis virus, three or four varieties of parasites, a host of toxic bacteria, and assorted nasty worms. My heart and liver were close to collapse, the doctors said, and my brain was riddled with parasites.

When I heard the words, "It's your brain, Dr. Villoldo," I sank into despair. The irony was, I had just published a book entitled *Power Up Your Brain: The Neuroscience of Enlightenment*. The doctors advised me to seek the best medical care available and immediately get my name on a liver transplant list. But where was I going to find a healthy brain?

After the conference, my wife, Marcela, was going on to the Amazon to lead one of our expeditions working with jungle shamans who have journeyed beyond death. I stood in the departure wing at the Cancún airport, staring at my options: Gate 15, the flight to Miami where I would be admitted to a top medical center for treatment, or Gate 14, the flight to Lima and the Amazon, where I would be with Marcela in the land of my spiritual roots. All my test results indicated I was dying; the doctors had even said, "You should already be dead." Miami was the logical choice. But in that moment I summoned up the courage to put my future where my mouth was—to live what I had taught to so many. My journal entry for that night reads:

> *Felt like it was the last day of my life. I was overwhelmed by sadness at the thought of leaving this beautiful earth, and I had to give a talk to 150 people! I knew I had to go to the jungle with Marcela. Otherwise I would be checking into a hospital in Miami, looking for my medicine in the wrong place. Now I*

am with the woman I love, returning to the garden where I first found my path.

In the Amazon, the shamans welcomed me lovingly. These men and women were friends who had known me for decades. And who knew me better than Mother Earth? She received me as only a mother can. As I pressed my body to hers, she spoke to me: "Welcome home, my son."

That night there was a ceremony with ayahuasca, a brew made from the *Banisteriopsis caapi* vine that shamans use for visioning and healing. I was too weak to participate and stayed in our hut near the river. Marcela went for us both. The bond that unites us is reflected in how we say *I love you* to each other: *"Desde siempre y para siempre"*—"Since the dawn of time and forever." I could hear the shaman whistling, and his haunting songs wafted across the river to me as I went into a light meditation.

Hours later Marcela returned smiling. Pachamama—Mother Earth—had spoken to her throughout the night: "I make everything on the earth grow. I am giving Alberto a new liver. He knows how to heal everything else." Pachamama was expressing her love for me and gratitude for bringing so many of her children back to her. In giving me a new liver, she was giving me life. The next day I wrote in my journal:

> *After morning yoga a luminous being appeared to me in broad daylight. She walked out of the river, and I saw her as if in a dream—a feminine spirit who touched my chest and told me that I was a child of the Pachamama and would live many more years, and that she would look after me, as my work on the earth is not yet done.*

My return to the Amazon was the beginning of a return to myself. But first there was an enormous amount of work to do. I was gravely ill. I had to become a traveler on a healing journey in a way that I had demanded of others. And I had to remind myself: *There are no guarantees here, Alberto. There is a difference between curing and healing. You may not be cured; you may die. But regardless*

*of what happens, you will be healed. You will not walk out of the jungle
into your old way of being.*

I could feel the life force draining out of me. When I gazed
into the mirror in the half-light of the Amazon dawn, I saw that
the luminous energy field around my body was thin and pale, not
glowing brightly as it should be. My face had the same gray pallor
I had seen on patients who were dying.

I wiped my day planner clean, cancelling every talk, every lec-
ture, every class. The first speaking engagement I cancelled was in
Switzerland, where the renowned Brazilian healer John of God was
on the program. I had never met John, but I knew the head of his
organization. A few days later I got a call offering me a distant-healing
session. Afterward, I wrote in my journal:

> *John worked on me with his entities, and I sensed a great
> spirit at the head of my bed. I could feel a tangle of ropes being
> removed from my liver, thick fibers being pulled out. Other enti-
> ties worked on my heart, while still others performed a spiritual
> "surgery" on my brain. It knocked me out. I could not get out of
> bed for the next 24 hours.*

From the Amazon, Marcela and I flew to Chile and our Center for Energy Medicine, where we conduct intensive workshops.
The monastery/retreat is in the Andes, near Mount Aconcagua,
the highest peak in the Americas. The mountain is the reason we
settled here. In the old Inca language, *aconcagua* means "where
you come to meet God." This is exactly what I needed. It was time
for the meeting I had been postponing for so long. I had only one
focus now—healing—and I had to be wholehearted about it.

My body was a road map of the jungles and mountains where
I had worked as an anthropologist, picking up the lethal critters
that had taken up residence inside me. The jungle is a living biology laboratory, and if you spend enough time there, you become
part of the experiment. I knew anthropologists who had died of
the diseases I now harbored.

Actually, the virgin rain forest of the Amazon is free of most
diseases, but to get to it you have to go through filth-ridden

outposts of Western civilization. The Indios knew better than to foul their nests and their drinking water. Meanwhile, the white man surrounded himself with a sea of garbage and sewage.

The spiritual medicine I received from the shamans was powerful, but I had to complement it with Western medicine. The doctors put me on a worm medication—the same type I give my dogs—and on antibiotics to kill other parasites. The problem was that the worms themselves harbored parasites, so when I killed the worms, they released *their* parasites into my brain, which became very toxic. The situation was dire. My brain was on fire with inflammatory agents and free radicals produced by the medications and the dead and dying parasites. I would have to detox my brain to avoid going completely mad.

My brain fog and confusion were glaringly evident when I tried to play *Scrabble* with Marcela. That game became the barometer of my mental health. I could not access words. And then I started losing my sense of self. I panicked: *What if I forget who I am? What if I lose my consciousness of self?* Madness stared at me from the horizon—I saw it, felt it, breathed it. It sent naked fear into every part of my being.

Ironically, it was fear of losing myself that saved me. Over the next three months, I simply observed the madness I was experiencing. The shamans (and Buddhists) have a powerful practice of self-inquiry that starts with asking, *Who am I?* Then, after a while, you begin to inquire, *Who is it who is asking the question?* So I began to ask, *Who is it who's going mad?*

There was no place to hide. I saw the madness; others saw it. But, as always, there was another side to the pain. The fathomless depths to which my spirit sank were matched by the flight of my soul. I began to understand who I had been since the beginning of time and who I would be after I died. The gnawing fear was matched by divine love. I dwelt in both worlds, belonging to neither. I wrote in my journal:

> *Buddha left the palace of his childhood after he saw death, disease, and old age. I have lived with these three grim reapers*

and have struggled to leave the palace of ignorance and arrogance that I built. I have surrendered to the pain and the ecstasy.

There is no way to adequately describe the place of darkness I reached, but the 16th century mystic John of the Cross must have understood it. From his prison cell he wrote: "There in the lucky dark, / . . . darkness far and wide; / no sign for me to mark, / no other light, no guide / except for my heart—the fire, the fire inside!"[1] I, too, was in a prison, with my soul on fire. I had a dream:

I am in our cottage, in a kind of cloister. I am waiting for a spiritual treatment. The healing by water is already done, but the one I am waiting for, the initiation by fire, is not ready yet.

I was the patient who should have died, and now I would have to look death straight in the eye if I wanted to live. I would have to draw on everything I had learned walking the shamanic path: all the healing practices, all the techniques for growing a new body by awakening stem cell production in the brain, heart, and liver.

I called my friend David Perlmutter, a renowned neurologist who was my co-author on *Power Up Your Brain*. Together we crafted a strategy using potent antioxidants to trigger the production of neural stem cells to repair my brain. What followed over the next months were countless Illuminations to clear the imprints of disease from my luminous energy field, along with intravenous infusions of the antioxidant glutathione to detoxify my liver, soul retrievals to recover parts of myself I had lost to trauma, and out-of-body experiences in which my spirit took flight into the Buddha fields, the *bardos,* the heavens. Energy moved, flowed, met obstacles, and flowed again. I was caught up in the highs and lows of fighting for my life. Time drifted by like a sluggish river, and I stepped out of it, knowing I had to make friends with eternity. In my journal I described one soul retrieval:

I strike the drum softly and journey to the lower world to attempt to do a soul retrieval for myself. I know it's not a good idea. The shaman who treats himself has a fool for a patient. But I know the Guardian, the Inca Huáscar, and he leads me to the chamber of wounds, where there is a pool of blood that triggers memories from my childhood of bloodshed in Cuba during the revolution.

I find a little boy who tells me his agreement with God is that he will never die, and that is why he cannot leave the hell he is in. I tear up that soul agreement and draft a new one that says, "Life and death and rebirth live within me." The child is happy and joins me. We then discover a ten-year-old boy, somber and serious, who explains that he must stay behind to look after the little one. The little one had received lifesaving blood transfusions at the age of two, when he got hepatitis C from a contaminated needle. I tell the ten-year-old that the little one is with me now, and the older boy smiles.

That night, I had another dream:

I am with friends looking at a grave full of flowers. I am buried there. My friends say I can stay there if I like. But I tell them I won't need this piece of earth. I see my soul rise from the ground.

I found solace in my dreams. But in spite of all the spiritual gifts I was receiving, my body still felt wretched. I feared I was exhausting all the life force that remained. This is the energy meant to be used at the end of life, in order to die consciously. As the *Bhagavad Gita* says, "Whatever the state of being / that a man may focus upon / at the end, when he leaves his body, / to that state of being he will go."[2]

I continually asked myself, *Where is my focus?* I could feel my mind teetering on the edge of the precipice. A journal entry reads:

Suffering is greatest when you believe you are at the end of your existence and face your annihilation. I have discovered the spiritual world, the continuation of life, and embraced it. Today I told myself, "I'm just going back home. It might be hard—birth

was not easy—but I'm going back home." I am blessed, for I
know the road. I have been shown the way so many times. In
shamanic ceremonies I have died a dozen deaths, have seen my
body rot and wither, and have gone to the stars. Heaven and
hell are both familiar. But just as the spirits did when I was two
years old, they're saying that my time is not yet.

This time, however, I knew I had a choice. I could choose to
remain in the world of Spirit. But the spirits were telling me that
my work was not done. I would have to return to ordinary life. My
mind led my body deeper into a state of collapse, and then into
my ultimate surrender. That's when I knew that something big
was about to happen. But first I had to visit the realm of the dead.
I dreamed:

> *Marcela and I are at a ferry terminal. There are many peo-*
> *ple waiting to board. We have a small boat just for us, one*
> *that belonged to my father. People help us launch our boat,*
> *which I know how to pilot because my father taught me. Not*
> *my human father, but the heavenly Father.*
>
> *I am preparing to cross the great water to the land of the*
> *ancestors in my own craft, not with all the others taking the*
> *ferry. I am making my journey to the land of the dead but not*
> *with the dying. I am going with my shaman wife.*

There it was: I had a new mission in life—to be a shaman. But
wait! Hadn't I answered the call to be a shaman a long time ago?
I'd even written a book about it: *Shaman, Healer, Sage*. But writing a book doesn't make you a shaman, any more than writing
a cookbook makes you a chef or having a spiritual library makes
you a spiritual adept. For years I had been a spiritual guide but
not a master. I was like the wilderness scout who can find his way
through the forest but knows little of the destination. I wrote in
my journal:

> *For years I was like Moses, helping others to the Prom-*
> *ised Land but not being allowed to enter myself. Now that has*

changed. I am already in the Promised Land. I have been allowed entry. And I discovered that the door has always been open, that it was my pride and anger and fear that had kept me out.

Now Spirit was offering me another lifetime within this one. I was being called to step fully into my destiny, this time without self-importance, without the subtle seduction of worldly accomplishment. The externals of my life might not change, but my attitude had to. A new contract with Spirit was required.

I felt liberated. I was free. That night, I dreamed:

I am inside a breathing machine and friends are saying good-bye. I am unable to move or speak, but I am in bliss. They turn off life support. I have to pull myself out of the breathing apparatus to come back to life. I realize I can find eternity without dying. I rip the tube out of my mouth and breathe. I am alive. I understand that miracles organize space-time for healing to happen.

That was followed by another dream:

I am leading a group on a tour bus. We come to a monastery with many empty rooms. In one room, there are some altars with candles on them. I light a candle, leaving some coins, and then walk down a spiral staircase carved out of rock. As it descends, the staircase narrows. I reach the ground, and as I squeeze through the exit, I realize that the group won't be able to fit through the opening. The meaning seems clear: I must find another, less traveled path. I need to go alone.

Again, I was at a choice point. I did not have to stay on earth; I could return home. The last time I had been offered this choice, I was just a child, scared and in pain, but now my fear of the Great Journey had passed.

And then I realized that I did not have to die literally. I could die symbolically. I could stay and heal myself so I could help and heal others. Once I made that choice, I began reinhabiting my ordinary senses. I felt my spirit sinking roots into my body once again. Awe and wonder returned, as my brain fog began to clear and I saw that stewardship of all life and the earth was my path.

My return to health lasted more than a year. My good friend Mark Hyman, a physician who wrote *The Blood Sugar Solution* and *10-Day Detox Diet,* helped me put together a nutritional plan for healing. It included green juices in the morning and superfoods and supplements that boost the body's self-healing systems and detox the liver and brain. I completely changed the way I eat.

Today, I'm fully recovered. More accurately, I'm *beyond* recovered. I'm a new person. My mind is functioning at a higher level than it has in decades. My brain is repaired, and so is my heart. And I have a new liver—not a transplant, but my own liver, fully regenerated.

In *Power Up Your Brain* I wrote about the science of neuroplasticity and how we can trigger the production of neural stem cells that repair the brain. During my health crisis I became my own experiment of one, in the process discovering that it's not just the brain that produces stem cells. Every organ in the body does, and we can learn to turn on these repair and healing systems to grow a new body that's healthier and more resilient. At the same time, I also drew on the energy medicine taught to me by the shamans, removing the imprints of disease from my luminous energy field and guiding my body toward optimal health.

I've been reluctant to share my healing journey until now. People tend to be skeptical of "miraculous" recoveries. When anyone asks, "What brought you back from the edge of death?" I usually say, "The grace of Spirit." That's true, but I know there's more to it than that. If grace were the only factor in getting better, we would all be in outstanding health. What brought me back from the edge of death was One Spirit Medicine—and you don't need a miracle to be healed by it.

One Spirit Medicine is based on ancient shamanic healing methods going back to our Paleolithic ancestors 50,000 years ago, backed by the latest breakthroughs in modern neuroscience. I first encountered these practices many years ago, during my fieldwork in the Amazon and the Andes. But these traditional practices are being confirmed today by what we're learning about the body and the brain. For the last decade, together with physicians Mark Hyman and David Perlmutter, I've offered this program to clients who come to our weeklong retreats for detoxification and healing. They leave with body and brain restored. Now, in *One Spirit Medicine*, I offer you an opportunity to grow a new body using the same techniques.

My health crisis was more extreme than most. But the fact is, we're all in a life-and-death struggle with the toxic forces of modern life that throw our health and well-being out of balance. Many of us feel stressed-out physically and emotionally, and wonder why, with all the antianxiety and antidepressant medications and relaxation techniques available, we don't seem to be able to fix the problem.

Meanwhile, obesity, diabetes, ADHD, autism, and Alzheimer's disease are increasing at an alarming rate. Close to 70 percent of Americans are overweight, and one in three children born in America today will develop type 2 diabetes by the age of 15. Fifty percent of otherwise healthy 85-year-olds are at risk for Alzheimer's disease.[3] Alzheimer's is being called type 3 diabetes, linked to a gluten-rich, wheat-based diet and a stressed-out brain.[4] And these are just a few of the diseases that are killing us prematurely and compromising our quality of life.

Our ancestors in the Paleolithic era, as well as many of the tribal cultures I have lived with in the Amazon and the Andes, did not, as we often assume, lead short and brutish lives. They enjoyed healthier life spans, fewer incidences of warfare and violent crime, and less stress than the people who came after them, including us. What accounted for their health and well-being? A primarily plant-based diet and One Spirit Medicine.

One Spirit Medicine can help you avoid the illnesses that are ravaging civilization today. The shamans of old were masters of prevention. You do not have to be gravely ill to root out physical, emotional, and spiritual suffering and restore balance to your life. Using the principles and practices offered in these pages, you can feel better in a few days and begin to clear your mind and heal your brain in a week. And in just six weeks you can be well on your way to a new body that heals rapidly and ages gracefully, and a brain that supports you in forging a profound connection with Spirit and experiencing a renewed sense of purpose in life. One Spirit Medicine can give you all that, just as it gave it to me.

HOW TO USE THIS BOOK

I've designed this book to take you through the steps of preparing to receive the healing of One Spirit Medicine. To get the most out of the process, I recommend reading the chapters in the order in which they're presented and trying the practices and exercises.

Part I: Discovering Your Inner Healer introduces One Spirit Medicine, outlining what this ancient healing system is and how it addresses the physical and mental challenges of modern life. You'll discover how One Spirit Medicine differs from Western medicine and what you will need to do to benefit from its healing power. You'll learn about the invisible world of radiant, living energy that informs the visible world of the senses, and about Spirit's role as the harmonizing force. You'll be introduced to the tyrannical mind-set that has dominated humanity since the dawn of agriculture and how it drives us to war with ourselves, with each other, and with the planet, undermining our health and well-being.

Part II: Shedding the Old Ways identifies the myriad environmental and endogenous toxins we're exposed to and explains why detoxification of the body and brain is essential for healing. You'll learn about the body's all-important "second brain" in the digestive tract and how to get rid of toxins in your gut and replenish the beneficial bacteria of your microbiome. You'll be introduced to superfoods and supplements that promote brain and gut repair. You'll discover the toxic effects of grains and sugars, and learn how fasting helps the brain to fuel itself on healthy fats and proteins and produce neural stem cells to repair and upgrade itself.

In **Part III: Overcoming the Death that Stalks You,** you'll address the dysfunctional mental and emotional patterns associated with anger and fear, and learn which nutrients improve higher-brain function and help you manage stress. You'll be introduced to the mitochondria, the power centers of your cells. Inherited only from the mother, they represent the feminine life force. You'll learn how to reset the cells' death clocks and switch on longevity proteins controlled by mitochondria. You'll find out what free radicals and inflammation do to the body and how to reverse the damage. And you'll discover traditional shamanic healing techniques that can clear your luminous energy field of the imprints for disease and upgrade it to repair your body and brain.

Part IV: From Stillness Comes Rebirth supports you in completing the process of letting go of old, unhealthy ways of thinking so that you can experience healing with One Spirit Medicine. You'll learn how to shed outworn narratives about your past and embrace a new, liberating personal story or mythology. You'll overcome fear of loss and change and discover the purpose of your life's journey as you're guided through the wisdom teachings of the medicine wheel. You'll learn practices for cultivating stillness and awareness, as you take the final step on the journey to One Spirit, the vision quest.

At the end of the book, we'll explore what happens after you receive One Spirit Medicine and how you can sustain the healing benefits for yourself and promote wellness for all beings and the earth.

PART I

DISCOVERING YOUR INNER HEALER

CHAPTER 1

MEDICINE OF THE SHAMANS

*You are only a few days away
from feeling well.*

Today our minds, our emotions, our relationships, and our bodies are out of kilter. We know it, but we tend to ignore it until something goes very wrong—a scary diagnosis, a broken relationship, the death of a loved one, or simply an inability to function harmoniously in everyday life. When things are a little bad, we read a self-help book or go to a workshop. When they're really bad we bring in experts to fix the problem—oncologists to address cancer, neurologists to repair the brain, psychologists to help us find peace and understand our family of origin. But this fragmented approach to health is merely a stopgap. To truly heal we need to return to the original recipe for wellness discovered by shamans—traditional healers—millennia ago: One Spirit Medicine.

In the West we have a disease-care system, and medicine recognizes thousands of ailments and myriad remedies. One Spirit Medicine, on the other hand, is a health-care system that identifies only one ailment and one cure. The ailment is alienation from our feelings, from our bodies, from the earth, and from Spirit. The cure is the experience of primeval Oneness with all, which restores inner harmony and facilitates recovery from all maladies, regardless of origin.

We all want our health span—the length of time we're in optimal health—to equal our life span. One Spirit Medicine is designed to ensure us optimal wellness by addressing the root cause of physical, mental, and emotional suffering rather than just treating the symptoms. The words *health* and *healing* come from the Old English *haelen*, the root of *whole* and *holy*. As your whole system comes into balance, your food will stop poisoning you, your body will begin to repair and heal naturally, your relationships will cease to be emotional battlegrounds, and your sense of separation from nature and Spirit will dissolve.

At the heart of One Spirit Medicine is an age-old practice called the vision quest, a carefully choreographed encounter with nature and the invisible world. Through fasting and meditation, a vision quest awakens the body's self-repair and regeneration systems and reconnects you to Spirit and your own deepest purpose. In the traditional cultures where I trained as a shaman, it is customary to seek vision in the wilderness. But the experience of One Spirit can take place anywhere—even in your garden or a big city park.

In rare instances, the encounter with Spirit is spontaneous, a bolt from the blue. But for most of us, receiving One Spirit Medicine is a process that requires careful preparation over time. Otherwise, the experience will most likely be fleeting—a sudden flash of insight or revelation, maybe a good story to tell over dinner with friends, but nothing lasting that will transform your life. Laying the groundwork for transformation requires both physical and spiritual action.

PREPARING THE BRAIN FOR ONE SPIRIT MEDICINE

In order to benefit from One Spirit Medicine, we need to prime the brain. Today's overcaffeinated, staccato, I-want-it-now lifestyle keeps us in a constant state of stress. We need to be weaned off the stress hormones that promote a fight-or-flight mind-set and start producing the brain chemicals that create health, serenity, and joy. The process begins with detoxification—ridding the brain of deadly toxins and reducing the stress hormones adrenaline and cortisol. The superfoods then repair the region in the brain responsible for learning, and help the pineal gland manufacture DMT, or dimethyltryptamine, a psychedelic compound that has been referred to as "the spirit molecule." DMT allows us to experience a state of Oneness and connection to all that meditators frequently report.

Physical preparation for One Spirit Medicine also involves switching to a diet rich in phytonutrients—plant nutrients. Used for healing since the Paleolithic age, phytonutrients not only help us repair and prime the brain but also create extraordinary states of health. These plants are loaded with genetic modifiers that switch on more than 500 genes that create health and switch off more than 200 genes that create disease. Phytonutrients restore our neurochemical balance, allowing us to begin treating ourselves and our loved ones according to our best intentions.

This exchange of the toxic for the nourishing, of the deadly for the life-giving, is essential to recovering our health and attaining optimal well-being. You can't heal your emotions if your brain is toxic from mercury or lead poisoning, or your mind is careening unstoppably because your brain has been damaged by childhood trauma or pesticides in your food. Ridding yourself of environmental toxins is essential to restoring physical and mental health. Another key for priming yourself physically to receive One Spirit Medicine is repairing your microbiome—the 600-plus species of beneficial bacteria living in your mouth, skin, and gut. One Spirit Medicine will help you repair your brain and body by switching on the longevity genes and returning the alchemical laboratory of the brain to its task of producing the bliss molecules that bring us closer to Spirit and nature.

PREPARING THE MIND FOR ONE SPIRIT MEDICINE

To experience One Spirit Medicine, you don't need to shake a rattle or beat a drum as shamans of old did, though doing so may help prepare your mind in the same way that putting on a costume and makeup helps an actor get into character. What you *will* need to do is quiet your too-busy mind, distracted by the ruckus of civilization, and return it to the wild. By returning to the wild I don't mean going to Yosemite Park or the Canadian Rockies but returning to your wild, undomesticated self—to who you are stripped of the trappings of roles and expectations, e-mails and To Do lists, the authentic *you* at your core. You will meet your infinite nature in the stillness of your inner world.

Superfoods and neuro-nutrients bring about changes in your brain that set you up for an extraordinary experience of higher consciousness, while mental preparation helps you let go of limiting beliefs and toxic behaviors. As you free yourself of outmoded stories about your past, One Spirit Medicine can infuse your being like a steady IV drip of healthy nutrients.

If you've attended my workshops or traveled with me to visit shamans in the Amazon or the Andes, you may be familiar with some of the ideas presented in this book. You may feel, therefore, that you're ready to experience One Spirit Medicine now, without any further work. But have you really done *all* the necessary physical and spiritual preparation? Even if you've been on a vision quest—or on many of them—each time is a brand-new experience, an opportunity to go deeper into your encounter with Spirit. Shamans always prepare themselves carefully to work with the extraordinary energies of the invisible world in order to create and sustain health and well-being.

BENEFITS OF ONE SPIRIT MEDICINE

After you've taken One Spirit Medicine, you will find it easier to dance between the visible, physical world of the senses and everyday tasks, and the invisible world of Spirit. You will be like the graceful jaguar, the balancing force of the rain forest who serves as an intermediary between the seen and unseen worlds as it journeys beyond death into eternity.

Whether you're suffering from a lifestyle-related disease, or you're physically, mentally, or emotionally drained by the demands of your life, One Spirit Medicine can help you feel better and develop a renewed sense of purpose. If you're willing to repair the alchemical laboratory inside your brain, you can fix health problems *before* they manifest in your body and experience wellness at every level of your being.

At the core of One Spirit Medicine is the idea that how we perceive the world "out there" is a projection of internal maps that shape our beliefs and guide how we think, feel, and behave. Stored as neural networks in the brain, these maps are the unconscious programs that drive our experience of life and the state of our health. We want to change the maps that consider a 50 percent chance of Alzheimer's a normal part of aging after 85, or rampant cancer and cardiovascular disease "normal." The key to optimum health is to upgrade the unconscious maps and limiting beliefs that have been driving us to a toxic lifestyle and relationships.

Years ago I asked an old man in the Amazon rain forest what he did to avoid the diseases of old age. "Simple," he replied. "Live a long and healthy life." I laughed and said he had not understood the question: I wanted to know how to avoid the diseases of old age. He smiled and repeated the same answer.

Today I understand what he meant. The practices that are an everyday part of the ancient shamanic way all support a long and healthy life. The super-nutrients described in this book can turn on the dormant antioxidant mechanisms in every cell, quench free-radical activity in the brain, and switch on the latent longevity genes that prevent the illnesses associated with old age. The spiritual teachings of the medicine wheel help us shed debilitating and disempowering stories from the past that keep us reliving old traumas and the health history of our ancestors. And the vision quest supports us in finding new guiding myths to help us heal body and mind, and recover our passion.

One Spirit Medicine is part of a new wellness model that doesn't rely on medication to fix physical problems or mood imbalances. Unlike many pharmaceutical and over-the-counter remedies, the medicine of the shamans carries no side effects or warnings written in fine print. It will not cause dependency. You will not have to beg your physician to write a prescription for it, or argue with your pharmacist over whether or not your prescription renewal has been approved.

In the West, we're accustomed to looking to doctors and experts to guide us in our healing, growth, and learning. Our schools, businesses, religions, and government are hierarchical. In the Amazon, however, there are no levels of management between us and Spirit. The shaman—the wise old man or woman—is honored as a healer but is not regarded as superior to other members of the village. The shaman is simply a skilled facilitator who interacts with both the visible and invisible worlds to help restore balance to body, mind, and soul.

The message of *One Spirit Medicine* is that you don't need to track down a shaman to find Spirit, or look outside yourself to find health. You only have to look within. That's where you will receive One Spirit Medicine.

The old man in the Amazon was right after all.

CHAPTER 2

SPIRIT AND THE INVISIBLE WORLD

*There is a sea of consciousness that is universal
even though we each perceive it from our own shore.
It is a world that we all share, that can be experienced by
every living being yet is seldom seen by any. The shaman
is the master of this other world. He lives with one foot in
the world of matter and one foot in the world of Spirit.*

Decades ago, I spent a summer doing research in the Amazon rain forest, paid for by a grant from a Swiss pharmaceutical giant that was hoping to find a bark or root that could become the next great cancer cure. After all, the jungle is nature's pharmacy, filled with exotic plants whose powers have yet to be discovered. I spent many months canoeing to villages that had seldom seen a white man, and wherever I went, I found there was no cancer, Alzheimer's, or heart disease, even among the elders of the community. Clearly, the indigenous peoples of the area knew something about health that we Westerners didn't know. What was their secret?

I returned home with my backpack empty, to the annoyance of my sponsor, who couldn't believe I hadn't brought back the key ingredient for a blockbuster drug that would make us all rich and save lives at the same time. I did return, however, with something I thought more valuable—insights from the Amazon healers who had taken me under their wing. I learned that there was a magic ingredient to health that could be found in the rain forest but would not fit in a backpack. The ingredient was One Spirit Medicine, and it could be found only in the invisible matrix of the universe we call Spirit. It took years of studying with indigenous healers before I began to comprehend how it works.

Once you've experienced Spirit, the invisible matrix of overlapping fields of consciousness and information, you recognize that the visible world of the senses, the physical world, is not the only reality. In fact, it's not even the dominant reality. The visible and invisible worlds are inextricably intertwined with almost mathematical precision, and once you've opened your eyes to this, you can dance between them like the shamans.

The ancients knew all about the two worlds. In the Hindu Vedas, the invisible world is called *akasha*, or the vastness of space—the field of wisdom that forms the substrate of the cosmos. While Western science holds that the cosmos is made up of energy and matter, indigenous peoples consider the cosmos a living, intelligent field they know as Spirit. The word *spirit* itself comes from *spiritus*, Latin for "breath."

VAST AND OMNIPRESENT SPIRIT

Spirit is a vast and invisible energy field that we join with to dream the world into being. It is not a deity with human whims, moods, jealousies, and temper tantrums like the Greek and Roman gods. Spirit does not ask you to sacrifice your firstborn child, or slay infidels, or destroy cities when their citizens have lost their way. Spirit is the creative matrix that keeps life in the cosmos evolving and renewing itself.

Spirit is always present in your life; you are an expression of its infinite awareness, manifest in flesh and blood. It holds all of creation. And as you and Spirit are inseparable, all of creation is within you as well. But your personal, individual awareness is merely a drop in the ocean of all consciousness. Unlike your mind, which thinks you're the center of the universe, your spirit is free of obsession with *I*.

Awareness of our individuality, which we value so highly in our world, dissolves when we're in the expanded and expansive state that allows us to experience the Oneness of the invisible world. And when we return to the visible world and ordinary consciousness, our everyday problems somehow seem less significant.

When we engage with Spirit, we discover that each of us has the ability to interact with the divine directly, experiencing its numinous power firsthand. When we call for help, Spirit responds with what we truly need, even if we do not fully comprehend the response at the time. And our relationship with Spirit is one of mutuality, so when Spirit calls, we have to be willing to answer the call, whether or not we understand what we're being asked to do, and whether or not we want to do it. Years ago, when my children were little, I remember telling Spirit that I would respond to my calling when they were a little older; I was using my children as an excuse to avoid my mission in the world. But if you put off responding to Spirit until some future time—when you have enough money, or enough time, or enough sleep—then the contract with Spirit is likely to fall short of your wishes or expectations.

A HARMONIZING FORCE

Most of us were taught that bad things happen because we have sinned—broken the rules established by a supernatural deity, somehow offended the gods. But as I learned from the Amazon shamans, Spirit is not a fickle deity who acts vindictively, or tests our loyalty, or seeks retribution if we make a mistake. In fact, Spirit is not a deity at all. Spirit is the great balancing force of life itself. It brings harmony, not punishment.

Misfortune and disease are simply an imbalance in the natural harmony. It occurs when we're disconnected from the wisdom of the invisible world, when we're living unconsciously, trapped in limiting and disempowering stories. When all we see is the material world, our survival instincts kick into gear. We mistakenly believe that the only way to avoid illness, conflict, or suffering is by fighting for survival and exerting power over others. But in fact, our greedy, selfish, manipulative actions lead to the very illness, conflict, and suffering we're trying so hard to avoid.

That's not to say that we are the authors of all of the misfortune that befalls us. Sometimes when we're suffering what we're experiencing are the consequences of an imbalance we personally had no part in creating. The Ebola virus is an example. This deadly virus was once contained within a ten-square-mile forest in Africa, but when the forest was cut down for lumber, the virus lost its natural habitat and quickly spread to animals and humans in the surrounding area. Many of the people who have died from Ebola had nothing to do with cutting down the forest, but they suffered mightily from it nonetheless.

Most microbes only harm us when our body is out of balance and our immune system isn't responding properly. You may not have the power to ensure that no deadly parasite will attack you, but you do have the power to prevent and correct imbalances in your body and your relationships with others. If you're living in imbalance, you're in a state of separation from Spirit. To dream a healthier, happier life into being, you need to correct your relationship to Spirit.

THE VEIL BETWEEN THE TWO WORLDS

In our quest for scientific explanations of the universe, we have forgotten about the invisible realm and what we can find there. It's where we find peace, free of the suffering that exists in the material world. But if the invisible world is so marvelous, why aren't we spending all our time there?

The shamans say that the reason we take on a physical body is to evolve and grow, to acquire emotional maturity and wisdom. To use a metaphor from physics, when we're embodied we're like an electron in a particle state, while in the invisible world, we're like an electron in a wave state. The particle state is our "local" nature—flesh and blood, sitting on a couch reading. The wave state is our "nonlocal" nature, in which we extend to the farthest reaches of the universe, at one with all things. When we die and leave this body behind, we return to our nonlocal nature, to the formless invisible world. But the shamans of old learned to experience their nonlocal selves without dying—to taste One Spirit while still in the everyday world.

In the invisible world, in our nonlocal state, encompassing all of creation, we don't have enough substance to contain our consciousness. The ancient Maya called the acquisition of consciousness in our wave state "acquiring the jaguar body." Their priests were known as the *balams*—individuals who had defeated death and in their nonlocal state, had developed infinite awareness and then had brought that wisdom back to their fellow villagers. This is why the jaguar is such a powerful symbol throughout the Americas, representing the ability to journey beyond death, steep in omniscience, and return to the land of the living. After the experience of One Spirit Medicine we understand that there never was a locked gate between us and the invisible world. The invisible world exists alongside the visible world, ever present and accessible. We can bring its wisdom into our world at any time, to provide healing and balance. In the visible world, we can infuse matter with Spirit.

13

Today, technology promises to bring us omniscience. The interface between our senses and our machines is moving us ever closer to having the ability to access all the knowledge in the world instantaneously. But this is not the kind of infinite awareness I'm referring to when I speak of experiencing One Spirit. By infinite awareness, I mean the ability to experience the totality of the cosmos firsthand, across the farthest reaches of space and beyond time. With this wisdom, we can heal our bodies and participate consciously in our evolution as a species.

The veil that stands between us and the invisible matrix is only a trick of consciousness created by our beliefs. It is said that we have to "see it to believe it," but the converse is also true: we have to believe it to see it. Otherwise, we don't grasp what's right in front of us. Our mind dismisses the information.

When the conquistadors first came to the Americas, the indigenous peoples on the coast of Mexico didn't see their wooden ships. Their scouts saw only the billowing white sails. The Indians weren't blind or foolish or crazy. Having no concept of such large boats, their minds simply erased what their eyes perceived. Research shows that our mental biases are so strong that we easily dismiss sensory information that doesn't fit with our preconceived notions about reality. A century and a half ago, doctors scoffed at the notion of viruses that caused infectious diseases. After all, they couldn't see the alleged "bugs," so how could the bugs be real?

The visible world, which seems to be the only reality, comprises not only physical phenomena but also our thoughts and emotions. Functional magnetic resonance image machines (fMRIs) can show what is happening inside the brain in real time when someone feels compassion, or thinks, *I'd love to have a piece of chocolate right now,* or remembers a favorite tune. Neuroscience is demonstrating that consciousness has physicality.

LUMINOUS ENERGY FIELD

But how does the invisible world of Spirit impact health and healing? Surrounding the physical body is a luminous energy field, or LEF, that informs our cells and genes and microbiome—the community of microorganisms in and on the body—how to live and act in harmony. The LEF is invisible to most of us, though there are people who see this energy as an aura, a halo of color around a person's body. With practice, anyone can sense this energy. Rub your palms together briskly for a few seconds, then very slowly separate your hands slightly and see if you feel heat or a kind of density in the air between your palms.

The LEF can be thought of as the software that instructs your DNA, the hardware, to grow and repair your body. Until you receive One Spirit Medicine, your LEF creates your body according to genetic instructions inherited from your parents. It replicates the physical conditions and the psychological stories and dramas that cut across generations. Despite our longing to see ourselves as different, better, and more enlightened than our parents, we tend to perpetuate their health challenges and emotional issues, repeating them in our own lives in one form or another. Unless we interrupt the cycle, we will live the way they lived and die the way they died.

When the wisdom in the luminous energy field diminishes—when the level of coherence degrades—it creates disharmony and disease in the body. The 90 trillion cells of our microbe colony start looking after their own survival instead of ours. Cancer cells forget to die and want to live forever. But when the quality of the LEF is upgraded through One Spirit Medicine, it creates health.

Years ago I was amazed to learn that 90 percent of the human body consists of bacteria that are alien to us. Only the remaining 10 percent of the body is made up of our own DNA. So does this mean that *I* am only that 10 percent? No. I am the energy field that organizes this amazing living colony that has a sense of self, of I-ness. The 100 trillion cells of my colony are kept humming in harmony and balance by the LEF, operating through my brain and nervous system. Nature made us this way, no doubt figuring that it was better to have one brain coordinating it all than to give each cell its own mind and the freedom to decide what is best for the whole colony. Rather than freedom, that would be a free-for-all.

The LEF, then, to the shaman, is that drop of wisdom consciousness that has acquired individual awareness. It mediates between your brain, where you experience yourself as a distinct individual with your own unique awareness, and Spirit, where we are all part of the One. And since the LEF is a biomagnetic field, it does not end where the body ends but rather stretches to infinity and the farthest reaches of the universe, diminishing in intensity, yet never vanishing altogether. Your LEF contains stars and galaxies within it.

The LEF consists of light and vibration, so whatever you dream in this field alters its vibration and determines what you manifest in your body and the outside world. If you don't upgrade the wisdom in your LEF and choose instead to stay stuck in the same old beliefs—*Mom ruined my life,* or *The stork dropped me off at the wrong home,* or whatever old program you habitually run—the wound remains unhealed, and you wind up ill, or with some other undesirable outcome. In Eastern thought, this cause-and-effect is known as karma. And being stuck in karma is not an optimal way to go through life. But when you take One Spirit Medicine and raise the quality or wisdom of your LEF, you can begin to express the genes for health and longevity, and live a more rewarding life.

It's much harder for us to raise the quality of the LEF today than it was 100 years ago, or 10,000 years ago, when our Paleolithic ancestors were alive. Because of the toxins in our brain and nervous system from pesticides and mercury, we can no longer readily experience unity with all creation. No matter how arduously we meditate or how many times we chant *Om,* the invisible matrix of Spirit seems to elude us.

YOUR ETERNAL NATURE

One Spirit Medicine opens the doors to this invisible matrix of wisdom where everything is intertwined, where every thought we have impacts every cell in our body and every molecule in the cosmos. Quantum physics offers us another apt metaphor in the phenomenon known as entanglement: particles are mysteriously interlinked in such a way that even if they are at opposite ends of the galaxy, if you change the direction in which one particle is spinning, the other immediately reverses its spin. At first scientists thought entanglement might be a demonstration of faster-than-the-speed-of-light communication. Later they understood that it was simply the nature of related particles. The high shamans of the Amazon and Andes that I studied with believe that entanglement is the nature of all of Creation, that we are all interconnected. That is why they—and many North American tribes—refer to all living beings as "all my relations."

When you experience One Spirit Medicine, you access what the psychiatrist Carl Jung called the collective unconscious, that aspect of your consciousness that participates in the shared awareness of all Creation, that recognizes your Oneness with all beings and with nature. How can you harm the earth or other beings when you and they are inseparable? Conversely, how can you not attend to your own healing if you care about your fellow beings? Once you've experienced One Spirit Medicine, the idea of looking out for number one at the expense of others is inconceivable.

The awareness that we exist in both the visible and invisible worlds at the same time brings the realization that everything in your life is something you've dreamed into being from the invisible matrix of energy. Much as you may hate to admit it, that includes any emotional pain and suffering you may be experiencing. Even the apparent schism between the visible world of the senses and the invisible matrix of energy is an illusion you've created, albeit a collective one we share as human beings.

Thinking that the physical world is the only reality is a helpful notion for operating in everyday life: it's not easy to work your way through a To Do list when you're in a state of Oneness, experiencing your wave nature. But once you experience your interconnectedness with the cosmos, what you put on your To Do list is likely to change, and your ability to complete the list without sabotaging yourself will almost certainly improve.

The LEF allows you to dance easily and fluidly between the two worlds and balance the doing of the visible world with the non-doing—the just-being—of the invisible world. You can choose whether to focus on everyday activities or to rest in unity with Spirit. Whatever you're doing or not doing, you can be fully present in the experience instead of wondering whether there is something better somewhere else. Once you receive One Spirit Medicine, your dreams cease to consist of fantasies that other people will change their behavior and attitudes. Instead, recognizing that in your wave state you are part of everything and everyone, you can leave others to live their lives as they wish, and concentrate on living your own life authentically and imaginatively.

AWAKENING YOUR INVISIBLE SELF

When we sleep, we are awake in our dreams. When we are awake, we are sound asleep in the invisible field where dreams happen. Dreams, meditation, deep contemplative study, music, and prayer are common ways of learning about the invisible timeless realm. But these experiences are often fleeting, vanishing as we make our way from the bed to the coffeemaker. When we dream, we are in a timeless world, one minute encountering our long-deceased parents, the next traversing some fantastic landscape. But when we wake, no matter how vivid the images, we often let them slip from awareness, not realizing their value. In the West, psychologists trained in dream analysis are just about the only people who understand the importance of the dream life. Yet the Amazon peoples I lived with and learned from would share dreams every morning, looking to them for answers to pressing questions or wisdom to be passed on to the village.

One Spirit Medicine gives you back your birthright—recognition of your true nature as both a spiritual being and a physical being, a wave and a particle. It does this by bringing awareness of your invisible self, a self devoid of body or form that resides outside of ordinary time. Have you noticed that in your dreams you never seem to have a physical body, never seem to bump into tables or chairs? In dreams, we are pure awareness. In the invisible world we are formless and self-less, within an expanse that is infinite and blissful. It is only in the visible world that we bump into tables, fall off cliffs, encounter suffering and disease, and of course where we learn and grow.

One Spirit Medicine can lead you to a better understanding of the invisible world and how it can benefit you in your life. As the visible and invisible realms dance between life and death, form and formlessness, the bridge spanning them is the LEF. It links our aging, dying existence with the self unfettered by the limitations of physicality or time. From the shamans I learned that there is only life after life, that death is simply a brief change in status from a visible to an invisible existence. One Spirit Medicine shows us how we can create health and alleviate suffering by connecting with the source of all in the invisible world.

Every human being wants to be happy—to avoid pain, disease, emotional suffering, mental anguish, and the stress of modern living. But when you're unaware that you have the capability of creating your everyday existence, power slips away from you, and you begin to see yourself as the victim of an unknown and frightening force.

With One Spirit Medicine, you have the ability to dream your world and your health into being. And you will not have to create your health alone. You always have a co-creator in Spirit. After you receive the gift of One Spirit Medicine, you'll be able to connect to the wisdom of the invisible world wherever you are, even in a crowded airplane or train.

CHAPTER 3

DETHRONING THE TYRANT KING

Know that the mind is mad.

In museums and at amusement parks, children are drawn to models of the fiercest of the dinosaurs, *Tyrannosaurus rex*. The *Spinosaurus* and *Giganotosaurus* may have been bigger carnivores, and *Diplodocus* and *Apatosaurus* were many times the size of *T. rex*, but he had the good fortune to have his brand established first—at the turn of the 20th century, Victorian crowds eagerly bought tickets to view the skeleton of this oddity. The fearsome dinosaur was given a name worthy of sending shivers down the spine of an eight-year-old and assigned a reputation that fulfills a mythological purpose: he represents the tyrannical king who will destroy us if we don't bow to his power. Although we now know the *Tyrannosaurus rex* probably had feathers, in our imagination he had a thick, impenetrable hide that made him an undefeatable predator.

The myth of the ferocious ruler also lives on in the large-cat house at the zoo. The sharp teeth and bold mane of the male lion impress onlookers as he yawns behind the glass. Even though we now know it's the smaller, sleeker female lion who does the hunting while her male partner looks on, the peering crowds ignore the informational card at the side of the exhibit and gaze in awe at the "king of the jungle."

T. rex and the male lion are symbolically powerful because the image of a formidable creature ruling over us is deeply rooted in the human psyche. The notion of a warrior-ruler has been internalized to the point that we think of the mind as the dominant force of our being, lording over our thoughts, feelings, body, and spirit. We're told from infancy that our large, complex brains are what separate us from the rest of the animal kingdom. The mind truly believes that it's in charge, running our thoughts and emotions, not to mention our lives. We believe that to change our habits, our addictions, our relationships, and our feelings, all we have to do is change our mind. And so we keep changing our mind—without fixing our relationships, improving our health, or healing our emotions.

One Spirit Medicine proposes a more reliable fix. By letting go of the illusion that the mind is the ultimate tool for creating health, abundance, love, and well-being, we free ourselves to access a more effective tool: a relationship with Spirit and the invisible world. One Spirit Medicine wakes us to the folly of the tyrannical mind and connects us instead to timeless healing ways.

That's not to say we can't enlist the mind to help us heal body and mind. The mind-body connection has long been acknowledged as a factor in wellness as well as illness. The mind I'm referring to is the domineering limbic brain, which believes it's in charge and in control, and lives in scarcity and fear.

To our earliest ancestors, the connection with Spirit was paramount, as it is to most indigenous groups today. During my early work in anthropology, when I studied unspoiled cultures that lived much like their Paleolithic forebears, I was surprised to find how present Spirit was in their lives. Many of their legends are about a heavenly being who walks the earth bringing wisdom. We can still communicate with this being in special places and states of awareness, they believe. One of these beings is Quetzalcoatl, the feathered serpent, Lord of the Dawn to the Aztec and Hopi. To the ancient Maya he was known as Kukulkan.

Quetzalcoatl is the ever-returning God, associated with Venus, the morning star. The legends say that he returns in every new era to bring renewal and knowledge. His legacy remains as an organizing principle on earth, in much the way that Christ's teachings to turn the other cheek and love thy neighbor as yourself remain as guiding principles today. Quetzalcoatl teaches that from Spirit flows all wisdom. Mortal existence is a temporary state, yet we have to cherish it and care for it, as it is extremely difficult to earn a physical body. (The Buddhists have a similar notion of human incarnation as a precious gift that we must honor and make good use of.) To the indigenous peoples I studied, everyday mortal life isn't the only and ultimate reality; the invisible realm of spirit is the primary reality, and the spiritual self is the enduring, real self. Spirit guides the medicine men and women I studied with to discover the plants that have life-giving powers—edible green plants that are rich in phytonutrients.

Our Paleolithic ancestors regarded green plants as their primary source of sustenance. What an extraordinary collaboration there is between human beings and the plant kingdom. We are perfect symbionts: oxygen, the waste product of plant respiration, sustains life for us humans, and our respiratory waste, carbon dioxide, sustains life for the plants. Plants turn sunlight into nutrient-dense foods we can use to nourish and heal ourselves. For our ancestors, survival in the wilderness was a natural outcome of respectful interaction with nature. Knowing which berries were nutritious and which were poisonous and where to find edible roots required humans to communicate with green life in a way unknown to most of us today. Back then there were no tests for hazardous ingredients other than sampling every potential food and hoping not to die from toxins. Today, indigenous people who are carrying on the tradition of respectful dialogue with nature will tell you that they know the qualities of plants not through trial and error but because the plants speak to them.

The ancient means of acquiring knowledge has been written off by science, which can't measure, contain, explain, or reproduce these results. The relationship between Paleolithic hunter-gatherers and nature was one of trust: they never doubted that the earth would help them procure what they needed.

So how did we lose this intimate connection with Spirit and the natural world? Anthropologist Jared Diamond traces it back 10,000 years to the agricultural revolution, when humans exchanged the fat-and-protein-rich Paleolithic hunter-gatherer diet for a diet based on grains. Diamond calls this dietary shift "the worst mistake in the history of the human race." It led to centuries of war and conflict, he says, and gave rise to society after society of cruel masters, ruthless warriors, and hapless slaves.

With a diet based on wheat, barley, rice, and maize—grains with a high glycemic index, or blood-glucose potential—our early ancestors were essentially living on sugar. As my colleague David Perlmutter explains in his bestseller *Grain Brain,* our bodies and brains are still suffering the health consequences of this dietary shift. A brain steeped in sugar is sluggish and dull, less able to access One Spirit Medicine than a brain fueled on fat. In Chapter 4, you'll discover more about grain as a toxin to the digestive system and brain, and about the harmful effects of gluten, a protein in wheat.

With the rise of agriculture came the notion that survival and security were paramount and depended on a powerful ruler who could rally forces to protect the land, the peasants, and the grain stores. Humans became fearful and warlike, no longer trusting Spirit or each other. Direct experience of the divine gave way to religions overseen by intermediaries between God and man.

One Spirit Medicine brings our connection to Spirit and natural forces back into the healing equation. To find peace within ourselves and live harmoniously with all beings on the planet, we need to shift our allegiance away from the tyrannical mind. We can't go back to the old ways of our Paleolithic hunter-gatherer ancestors, but we can reclaim their way of experiencing the cosmos. And we need this to upgrade our neural circuitry if we hope to achieve wellness.

REWIRING YOUR BRAIN

During my journeys in the Amazon I noticed that the shamans used three distinct types of plants for healing. The first is what I call the aspirin tree. If you had a headache or a fever from malaria, you went to the aspirin tree—a white willow or a cinchona—and prepared a remedy from the bark. You wanted to get rid of the headache or reduce the fever. This is the kind of medicine that we practice in the West: we find a remedy to treat the symptom.

Another category of plants the shamans used is more reflective of how One Spirit Medicine operates. These are plants that switch on the body's natural regeneration and healing systems. They turn on the longevity proteins inside the cell, and detoxify the neurons. Among these healing plants are the cruciferous vegetables and spices like turmeric and black pepper. We'll explore these superfoods in detail in Chapter 5, as they are cornerstones of One Spirit Medicine.

The third category of healing foods consisted of those the shamans used to repair and nourish the brain. These remedies, which help activate the neocortex, the brain's higher centers, include plants like cat's claw and omega-3-rich foods. Today there is a wealth of scientific research exploring the benefits of omega-3-rich supplements to repair the brain, prevent dementia, and treat conditions like ADHD.

We don't need to bargain with a sorcerer or a witch for the elixir of One Spirit Medicine, or fly to the Amazon for a shamanic healing. We can upgrade the brain here and now, switching on circuitry that overrides fear-based programming and quiets the tyrannical mind.

THE LIMBIC BRAIN AND NEURAL NETWORKS FOR FEAR

When the mind is behaving tyrannically, it's running unconscious software belonging to the ancient limbic brain. The limbic brain is focused on survival, and when we're in its grip we see danger everywhere and respond like a trapped animal. Often known as the mammalian brain, the limbic brain is driven by the Four Fs—feeding, fighting, fleeing, and fornicating. These primitive survival programs are activated when we fuel the brain on processed grains and sugar. The limbic system is the same region of the brain that craves sweet comfort foods when we're feeling sad or insecure.

The limbic brain's obsessions with food and sex, its craving for mind-dulling drugs, and its bias toward aggression, emotional withdrawal, and other destructive behavior can be overridden by the neocortex, the "new" brain, which allows us to learn, create, envision new futures, and make plans. The neocortex is programmed for beauty, whether it's found in a Mozart concerto or an elegant mathematical solution.

The neocortex thrives on One Spirit Medicine; the limbic system, driven by sensation, pleasure seeking, and emotion, does not. The new brain needs good fats to run at its best. Otherwise it merely sputters along, coughing up the occasional brief revelation but no lasting insight. The new brain doesn't fare well under stress. When we're stressed, it leaves the limbic brain in the driver's seat. The problem is that the limbic brain evolved when we were sitting quietly by the river's edge or watching the sun set lazily over the African savannah. It is not used to the rhythm of the world today. It can become so overstimulated that it hijacks the entire neural apparatus. Blood flow to the front of the brain, where we perceive opportunity and come up with creative solutions to problems, is then reduced. Raw emotion overtakes us, and we become blind with jealousy or rage, paralyzed with fear, or so riddled with anxiety that we can't think straight.

Often we're not even aware that we're operating out of beliefs programmed into the limbic brain. Survival oriented, these beliefs center on fear and violence: the world is a dangerous place; there are tigers around the corner waiting to eat us; there aren't enough resources to go around; death means the end of our existence. Beliefs like these become etched into the neural networks in the brain.

Neural networks are information superhighways that process what we perceive and feel. They tell us red means danger, green means go, who is sexy, who is dull. They hold a dynamic map of our world and how our reality works. This map contains sights, sounds, scents, memories, and early childhood experiences. It is thought that as many as half of our maps of reality are formed in the womb, as the mother's stress hormones pass through the placental barrier to the fetus. So if your mother was not sure she could count on your father to be there and support her, your map will code for a reality in which you can't count on men to be there for you, or a universe where men will not support your endeavors. If, on the other hand, your mother was confident she could count on her beloved, your mental map will show a world you can count on—and it will create this reality around you.

These neonatal neural networks are strengthened as your day-to-day experience proves your mythic map true, with more connections between neurons formed every time that pathway is used. Over time, this becomes the path most traveled and eventually the only route. A brain scan will actually show the breadth of neural networks in a particular area of the brain. The opposite is true as well: When a neural network falls into disuse and is pruned away, the void in that area of the brain will show up on a scan. So even if you have a spiritual awakening during a weekend meditation retreat, unless you make a conscious effort to continue practicing once you return to your everyday cutthroat existence, the epiphany will fade away. It's not easy being a Zen monk in corporate America.

Our neural networks make us creatures of habit. We stop having innovative thoughts and original perceptions very early on. In fact, most of our neural networks are set by age seven, when we stop drawing purple pigs and imagining houses in the clouds and in the roots of trees. Adverse childhood experiences not only affect development but also correlate with higher levels of alcoholism, heart disease, depression, teen pregnancy, and many other negative behaviors later on.[1]

Just as we develop practical neural networks for everything from reading and speaking to riding a bicycle and being polite, childhood traumas form networks for fear, anger, suffering, and abandonment that are encoded in the limbic brain. We repeat the underlying themes of these experiences, even if we don't recall the events themselves. As I reflect back on my own life I notice that I have always suffered around the same themes—lost love, hurt, and abandonment. And fear. When I moved to New York City for a summer decades ago, I arrived at my new apartment on a hot and muggy day. A bunch of beefy guys in sweaty T-shirts were sitting on the front steps. I was convinced I'd moved into a neighborhood of muggers and killers. Later, I discovered the guys were my neighbors and couldn't have been nicer. I had unknowingly superimposed childhood memories of the Cuban Revolution on these innocent neighbors.

Often themes run in families, passed down from parent to child. In the Amazon, they call this a generational curse. It can trigger the genes for disease. An emotional pattern may manifest as a physical ailment. Autoimmune diseases, which involve the immune system attacking its own cells, often run in families with poor emotional boundaries: family members have trouble acknowledging what is yours and what is mine.

Whatever willpower we exert to change our habits, we often fall back into the old themes because of our ever-efficient neural networks. The good news is that we can rewire the brain for joy and more nourishing outcomes.

NEUROPLASTICITY

Neuroplasticity, the notion that our experiences and perceptions affect the brain's functioning and structure, is a relatively new discovery, but it matches what sages have known for millennia about how the mind shapes the physical world, including the brain. That's why it's so important to upgrade and nourish your brain so that it can access One Spirit Medicine.

And experiencing One Spirit Medicine in itself alters the brain. Awakening to Oneness, to immersion in divine creation, can help you change lanes in the information superhighway in your brain so that you see the world with new eyes. After taking One Spirit Medicine, it's easier to shed old stories and write new, more interesting and beneficial ones.

The neural networks act like filters that screen out certain experiences, allowing us to perceive only a limited slice of reality. So, like the old Aztec scouts we will fail to notice the conquistadors' ships, which later seem so obvious to us. We may fail to read the emotional warning signs from the person we are dating, before we become entangled in a toxic relationship.

These networks also create self-fulfilling prophecies. If you believe the world is full of thieves and liars, then that is what you will encounter. Talk therapy isn't effective in dismantling stories scripted during childhood trauma when, instead of helping us write a better story, it only reinforces the old one.

One Spirit Medicine works by upgrading the information in your luminous energy field, eventually allowing new neural networks to form. Infusing the LEF with fresh energy and wisdom, One Spirit Medicine clears out stagnant, dark energies that harbor unconscious memories of past hurts. As the rewritten story is encoded in the field, it lays down new, more positive networks in the brain.

Once you've taken One Spirit Medicine, you will find it easier to slip into stillness and awareness of your primeval nature. Experiencing the invisible world of Spirit whenever you wish, you will be aware of the vast resources available to you to craft a healthy and creative life.

PART II

SHEDDING THE OLD WAYS

CHAPTER 4

DETOXIFYING THE GUT-BRAIN

I listen to my stomach and force myself to meditate on its groans. It's a lot easier to fast when you know there is food available around the corner. I imagine I can see the walls of my stomach rubbing against each other, muscles straining, and each contraction brings up a forgotten image from my childhood: mother, father, beach, happy. Father gone. Scared. Alone. Adolescence, love, lies, conceit, and deceit are all rolled into one. Who do I pray to for forgiveness when I no longer believe in anything?

Hiram Bingham was the discoverer of Machu Picchu, and I have chosen to retrace his footsteps through the jungles of Peru to the mythic Inca City of Light. It's curious that when a "civilized" man is shown a place where natives have lived for centuries, he is called its discoverer—as if the natives had been keeping it a secret from the rest of the world.

Now I am camping at a cave just below the deserted ruins. Fasting for three days before I enter the citadel. Otherwise, the shamans tell me, I will miss the "spiritual" Machu Picchu. All

I would see would be a pile of stone, not the invisible city that overlies the ruins. Will I be able to see through the mist, part the veils of this ancient palace?

And why do I have to do it on an empty stomach? The old man said, "So you can meet the beast within you and leave it outside the ruins." The beast turns out to be my entire past: the search for glory disguised as adventure, the ego rewards of revealing the treasures of ancient cultures to the world. The beast is me.

All the loose ends, all the polluted relationships, all the sorrows and joys—amazing what rises to the surface when you stop eating three meals a day, even for just a couple of days. I know that even on my lean frame, I have enough body fat to live off for months. But hunger is a great teacher. No wonder the psychology of the West is oral and anal.

—JOURNAL

Consider this: You have a second brain in your gut, and it's every bit as important as the brain in your head. This second brain is a network of more than 100 million neurons that communicate directly with the brain in your head. The neurons form a latticelike sheath surrounding the entire alimentary canal, or digestive tract—the nearly 30-foot-long tube running from your mouth to your anus. This sheath isn't concerned with poetry, love, philosophy, or whether there's life after death. Its main preoccupation is the daily grind of digestion: breaking down food particles to extract the nutrients, absorbing those nutrients, and then eliminating waste. It's an enormous job, yet all this neural firepower isn't dedicated exclusively to digestion and elimination. The vagus nerve—the longest of the cranial nerves—snakes up through the body from the gut to the brain, carrying a variety of vital information.

So, what kind of information does the gut-brain send to the brain between your ears? And how does this information relate to your moods, your feelings, and your "gut instincts"?

The gut-brain produces—and uses—95 percent of the serotonin in the body. Serotonin is both a hormone and a neurotransmitter. It plays a crucial role in developing our forebrain, which processes our emotions. Serotonin also enhances the growth of new neurons in the hippocampus, the part of the limbic brain that regulates the fight-or-flight system. The hippocampus enables us to have new experiences and learn from them. Both the forebrain and the hippocampus have to be functioning optimally for One Spirit Medicine to work, but that's largely because of yet another important role serotonin plays.

Serotonin is converted at nighttime into melatonin to signal the brain that it's time to release ordinary reality and enter the magical realm of dreams. It is a hormone found in plants, animals, fungi, and bacteria, and probably the most ancient and universal hormone in the evolution of life on earth. Serotonin is also known as the "feel good" or "happiness" hormone. It is chemically analogous to DMT, "the spirit molecule." DMT can be synthesized by the pineal gland in the brain—and it is found not just in the human brain but ubiquitous in nature; most plants and animals have it. DMT is also a component of hallucinogens traditionally used by indigenous peoples of the Americas, including ayahuasca, a psychedelic concoction brewed up by Amazon healers as an aid to visioning and healing.

Today, DMT is a doorway for seekers in the Western world who are venturing into spiritual territory that was once the exclusive domain of shamans and other native psychonauts. "DMT can . . . really open up the layers of your ego," explains Mitch Schultz, director of the documentary DMT: The Spirit Molecule, about psychiatrist Rick Strassman's pioneering research on DMT and spiritual experience. "Pulling back those layers of the ego, you start to get a sense of that perfect awareness of your being. And to me that is more real than real, if you will. More real than this hallucination that we're living in on a daily basis."

Clearly, DMT plays an important role in attaining the states of consciousness associated with One Spirit Medicine. I believe that nature designed the brain to allow serotonin to be turned into DMT by the pineal gland, granting us access to higher consciousness and direct perception of our interconnectedness with all creation. This is another compelling reason to attend carefully to the health of the gut-brain, where our serotonin is manufactured.

WESTERN MEDICINE IGNORES THE GUT

Western medicine is using its best efforts, including medications and surgical procedures, to limit the ravages caused by our poor eating habits and sedentary lifestyles. But at the same time, it virtually ignores the body's remarkable ability to heal itself. According to the Kaiser Family Foundation, 90 percent of Americans over 65 rely on at least one prescription drug to treat an ailment.[1] We have thousands of medications to address symptoms but almost none to address the underlying causes of the imbalances that lead to disease.

Research now shows that most of the diseases of modern living begin in the gut and are related to our diet. The gut-brain is a superhighway with many lanes of information traffic going in either direction between the brain in the head and the brain in the belly. Mental and emotional stress triggers physical responses that affect the gut, while disturbances in the microbiome—the colony of microorganisms in the gut—affect the functioning and health of the brain. When the gut colony becomes unbalanced, with more harmful microorganisms than helpful ones, the flora in the belly begin to produce toxins that wreak havoc with the immune system, alter brain function and mood, and weaken immune defenses.

I recently took my mother to the doctor, and the first thing he asked her was, "What medications are you taking?" In the West, if you're suffering from anxiety, brain fog, or depression, most physicians or psychologists aren't going to ask what foods you're eating, or pay attention to the balance between beneficial and nonbeneficial flora in your gut. And if you have GI disturbances, it's unlikely that your gastroenterologist will ask about your mental and emotional stress. When it comes to fixing the gut-brain, Western practitioners are just beginning to catch up to what the ancients knew. The same day I took my mother to the doctor, I took my dog to the veterinarian, and the first thing she asked was, "What do you feed your dog?" I decided that if I got sick again I would make an appointment with my vet.

In recent years, neuroscience has confirmed that our thoughts, beliefs, and feelings influence the physical structure of the brain. Once you've returned your brain to a state of optimal functioning, it becomes easier to make conscious changes in your habits and lifestyle. Even if you're one of the rare people who claim to be handling stress fairly well, you still definitely need to upgrade your brain.

Do you sleep well? Can you recall your dreams in the morning when you wake up? Are you able to dream lucidly, knowing you're dreaming while you're in the dream? Do you learn rapidly? Are you able to adapt to new situations easily? Are you able to leave work stress in the office and not take it home? If you answered no to any of these questions, you need to upgrade your brain.

TOXINS THAT DEGRADE BRAIN FUNCTION

Every day, toxins inside and outside the body damage our gut-brain. They come from the foods we eat, the water we drink, the air we breathe, even from the earth itself: contaminated soil pollutes plants and the water supply. Our bodies contain over 600 varieties of microbes from nature—including what one researcher calls "a virtual zoo of bacteria"—outnumbering by ten to one the cells that are strictly native to us, containing our own DNA. The colonies of flora in our skin, mouth, and gut need to live harmoniously with one another.

We're designed to routinely ingest microorganisms from the environment—to be in a continual exchange of bacteria with the earth, sky, air, and water. As a fetus in your mother's womb, you're microbe-free. Then, as you make your way down the birth canal, you begin to acquire the millions of microorganisms that make up your microbiome. This is one reason mother's milk is so important to babies: newborns pick up microbes around the nipple that become part of their intestinal flora. Later, more microbes enter your gut as you begin to explore the world—gumming your toes, being kissed by your parents and licked by the family dog, stuffing food into your mouth with filthy fingers. A microbiologist friend recently suggested that the reason humans kiss is so the bugs can test to see if they're going to get along with one another!

And while we have a dozen or so square feet of skin, we have more than 3,000 square feet—approximately the size of a tennis court—of gut surface that is constantly tasting the environment through the foods we ingest. In fact, the primary way we engage with the environment is through our gut, not our hands or skin. The GI system isn't supposed to be sterile; it won't work properly unless we have enough of the right flora in our gut. But every time we take an antibiotic drug we are in a sense "nuking" all the gut flora, the friendly as well as the bad, decimating their population. Small wonder so many of us have digestive and immune disorders: our guts are overwhelmed by the toxic load we've placed on them.

Upgrading your gut-brain—your digestive system *and* the brain in your head—requires that you detox your body to remove harmful toxins.

ENVIRONMENTAL TOXINS

Today, environmental toxins make up an overwhelming percentage of the toxins in our bodies. We are assaulted by pesticides, industrial chemicals, preservatives—even medication flushed down the toilet that makes its way into the community water table. There are over 80,000 industrial chemicals in use today that were unknown 100 years ago. Burning fossil fuels and disposing of manufacturing waste have added even more contaminants to our living environment, increasing our toxic load.

Our ancestors were largely protected from such challenges. For hundreds of thousands of years, the earth was able to accommodate changes brought about by human intervention. Our impact on the land we roamed over and the waters we fished was relatively minor, creating no permanent damage to the ecosystem. We lived sustainably: our food was organic, our waste was easily recycled, and we built homes of natural materials like mud and straw. We didn't have genetically modified foods, or plastics with a half-life of 10,000 years, or nail polish laced with formaldehyde.

All that changed, however, as we started to mine natural products like lead and mercury, and introduce them into our homes—and bodies—through everyday products like paint, bathtubs, light bulbs, lead pipes, and dental fillings, and more recently through contaminated fish and seafood. Mercury is a known neurotoxin, and both lead and mercury have been implicated in developmental problems like learning disabilities and ADHD. (The expression "mad as a hatter" is said to refer to the mental disorders suffered by millinery workers who were exposed to mercury vapors in the manufacture of felt hats, a common practice in the 18th and 19th centuries.) Metals like lead and mercury are stored in body fat, and nearly 60 percent of the brain is made up of fat.[2]

And heavy metals are not the only environmental pollutants that impact our health. In the last century or so, we've released thousands upon thousands of man-made chemicals into the environment. Molecules synthesized in the laboratory comprise everything from pesticides, flame retardants, clothing, shampoos, nonstick cookware, electrical appliances, and plastic water bottles to chemicals used in mining and manufacturing, and even in medicine and drugs. Data on how these chemicals affect us are scarce: of the 82,000 chemicals approved for use in the United States, only a quarter have been tested for their effect on humans. But none of these molecules can be ingested by insects or bacteria and then recycled into a substance that the human body or the environment can use. (There's a reason fast-food French fries don't lose their color or shape when they sit for months underneath a car seat in the family SUV: no self-respecting microbe would have anything to do with chemically saturated food.)

The regrettable consequence is that most of the chemicals we manufacture remain in the environment in their original form. We have older buildings filled with toxic lead-based paint, and carcinogenic chemicals are contaminating the sludge on the bottom of rivers that flow past polluting factories. Pharmaceuticals we toss in the garbage or flush down the toilet join the mix of toxins in the earth, water, soil, and air. Among the most ubiquitous contaminants in the U.S. are flame retardants, which saturate virtually every manufactured product we ever encounter, in virtually every setting. Flame retardants are surface coatings: as microscopic particles flake off, they bind to dust and are circulated through the air. Researchers have found flame retardant in an array of popular foods on the supermarket shelves, including butter and peanuts. Even more disturbing, they've found flame retardants in mother's milk.

As harmful molecules circulate, they're inhaled or eaten or drunk or absorbed through the skin, wreaking damage before they're excreted back into the environment in a never-ending toxic cycle. And we humans are not the only beings affected. Killer whales that recently washed up in the Georgia Strait were so filled with PCBs and other toxins that the whales were declared a health hazard and treated as toxic waste.

The human brain is not designed to handle the toxic overload that has been released into the environment. This is not news for many of you reading this book. What is new is our understanding that these neurotoxins prevent us from attaining the state of One-ness so easily reached by our Paleolithic ancestors—the conscious-ness required to create health.

GENETICALLY MODIFIED FOODS

The havoc we've created with man-made chemicals reverber-ates throughout the food chain. But it may be matched by an-other, even more insidious threat in the foods we eat every day. Much of the toxic overload in our guts comes from genetically modified foods. In most cases, we don't even realize toxins are on the menu. Scientists are increasingly altering the DNA of foods and food crops to create products that will last longer, be more resistant to disease and pests, and look and taste better. You may have noticed that at farmers' markets, bruised apples are slower to move than their shiny, unblemished display-mates.

Plants can't flee from their enemies, so nature equipped them to synthesize chemicals that repel predators. But more than 90 percent of the corn grown in the U.S. contains a genetically modi-fied gene that allows the plants to produce an even more powerful insecticide. Bugs that attempt to eat the corn are killed instantly as their stomachs burst open. The gene spliced onto corn—and cotton crops—is from *Bacillus thuringiensis* (Bt) bacteria. The food industry claims that Bt toxin poses little threat to humans or an-imals: it is rapidly destroyed in the stomach, they say. Yet mice exposed to Bt have shown dramatic effects, from allergic reac-tions to intestinal damage, and farm workers in India who handle Bt-modified cotton have had allergic reactions that include sneez-ing, runny noses, and watery, itchy, burning eyes.

Bt toxin is now found in nearly 85 percent of all streams and waterways in America, and more than 90 percent of pregnant women tested showed Bt toxin in their blood. Clearly Bt isn't co-operating with the industry's claims, increasing the likelihood that it will be around long enough to have lasting effects on our food supply.

Soybeans are another crop that is frequently genetically modified. Monsanto's Roundup Ready Soybeans are engineered to tolerate the pesticide Roundup. Scientists are now finding that the genetically modified proteins in corn and soy are inserting their genes into the DNA of the friendly bugs in your intestines, where they continue to function long after you've stopped eating the soy or corn.

Genetically modified tomatoes, squash, and sugar beets are commonplace today. And we find genetically modified foods not only in the produce aisle but also in sections of the supermarket where we would least suspect, like the fish department. In fact, more than 70 percent of all foods on the grocery store shelves contain a food substance that has been genetically modified. Unless you eat foods clearly marked "Certified organic by the USDA," you are taking part in a genetic experiment that is unprecedented in earth's long history.

TOXIC EFFECTS OF GRAIN

Genetic engineering isn't the only way in which toxins from food can harm the gut-brain. Globally, we're faced with new diseases caused by widespread reliance on a grain-based diet. One of the problems is that the wheat we're eating is not the wheat people ate even 75 years ago. To eliminate famine in places like the Soviet Union, the post–World War II green revolution introduced a high-yield dwarf wheat containing 20 times more gluten than the old European strains, thereby altering the composition of the bread we're consuming. (Gluten is a protein that gives dough its elasticity.) The dramatic increase in celiac disease—a debilitating autoimmune disorder in which ingesting gluten damages the gut—is likely related to this major change in our diets.

Whether or not you're among those who suffer from celiac disease, the harsh truth is that we *all* have become gluten intolerant to a surprising degree. Gluten is found in most grains, including wheat, rye, and barley, but the human digestive system hasn't evolved to function well on a grain-based diet. So grains have become toxic to many of us, and our grain-rich diets are damaging the gut-brain.

Carbohydrates from grain break down into glucose, which can serve as fuel for the brain. But carbs are not the best fuel. The higher-order circuits in the human brain evolved to run on fats. When the brain is fueled by sugars from grain, it reverts to a primitive, predatory survival mode, adversely affecting our moods, mental functioning, and overall health.

TOXIC EFFECTS OF SUGAR

The most deadly toxin found in nearly every kitchen cupboard in America is sugar. The typical American adult consumes 150 pounds of added sugar a year, including fake sugars like aspartame, saccharine, and sucralose, and high-fructose corn syrup.[3] Processed foods are sources of much of this amount. Even foods we don't think of as sweet—like catsup, peanut butter, and yogurt—often contain sugar or sugar substitutes.

You may think that putting Splenda in your tea is a healthier choice than using natural sugar, but artificial sweeteners can be even more harmful to the brain and gut. Fake sugars confuse your brain by making you crave something to eat even when you're not really hungry. And then you satisfy your cravings with sugars and grains, the very foods that feed yeast, fungi, and bad bacteria in the gut, and lead to weight gain. The use of artificial sweeteners has even been linked to type 2 diabetes.

Sugar in all forms except honey also reduces your levels of BDNF, brain-derived neurotrophic factor, a hormone that triggers the growth of new neurons and stem cells in the brain, repairing crucial brain structures. It is even thought that the connection between diabetes and Alzheimer's—a hot topic these days—is attributable to the typical Western diet high in sugar.[4]

Food cravings—particularly for sugary junk foods—are a common response to emotional upset. Your lover dumped you or you've had a setback at work, and what do you reach for? A chocolate-chip cookie perhaps, or more likely the whole bag. But food cravings aren't just a psychological problem, all in your head; they're in your gut-brain as well.

You may think that you're gorging on chocolate cake or tortilla chips because you love the taste, but the real reason you can't eat just one is that the yeast, fungi, and bad bacteria in your gut thrive on sugar, and to get their fix they bring on carb or sugar cravings. When lab rats that have been addicted to cocaine are given a choice between cocaine and sugar, 100 percent of the time they choose sugar. Sugary foods and carbohydrates stimulate the same centers in the brain that are stimulated by drugs like heroin and cocaine. They release the neurotransmitter dopamine, triggering a pleasure response, so you associate the food with pleasure, and then, wanting more pleasure, you eat more of the food. The cycle continues, and you become addicted to comfort foods.

Whenever you give in to your cravings and reach for a cookie or a breakfast muffin or a plate of pasta, that means the bad bacteria are winning the battle for your gut.

ENDOGENOUS TOXINS

Not all the toxins affecting the gut-brain come from food or the environment. Toxins are released inside the body by the "bad" microbes in the gut and by the breakdown of hormones. The microbes eat and eliminate waste just as we do, and toxins they produce can affect the brain and other organs.

Henry Lin, a researcher at the University of California's Keck School of Medicine, has mapped out a new way of thinking about how toxins in the gut affect the brain. According to Lin, a bacterial imbalance in the small intestine, caused by wayward bacteria migrating from the large intestine into a normally bacteria-free region,[5] triggers a response in the immune and nervous systems that can lead to insomnia, anxiety, depression, and impaired cognitive function. The gut's immune system signals the brain to produce high levels of CRF, or corticotropin-releasing factor, which triggers increased levels of the stress hormone cortisol and the neurotransmitter dopamine, and reduces serotonin levels.

WHAT HAPPENS IN THE GUT DOESN'T STAY IN THE GUT

It's clear that what happens in the gut affects the whole body. A healthy gut is filled with trillions of friendly intestinal flora that help you digest food properly, extract all the nutrition from it, and manufacture vitamins. Among other things, these bacteria synthesize vitamins B, C, and K, leading early investigators to call the gut microflora collectively "the forgotten organ." Good bacteria in the gastrointestinal tract help reduce cellular inflammation and keep toxins in check. They also play an important role in creating and maintaining the mucosal immune system in your gut. They even train your immune system to tell the difference between pathogens—microorganisms that make you sick—and nonharmful antigens that help you fight disease. Maintaining this balance prevents your immune system from overreacting to certain antigens, causing allergies.

The good bacteria are supposed to far outnumber the bad bacteria in the gut. And it's not just grains and sugar that disturb the balance of flora in the gut. Hormones, antibiotics, and other drugs in nonorganic meat, poultry, and dairy also encourage the growth of yeast and bad microbes and lower the amount of good bacteria. Recently, there's been a big increase in the number of people with a debilitating form of colitis known as *Clostridium difficile*, or C-diff, that's linked to an imbalance in the gut caused by antibiotic use.

Clinical research has found that people whose digestive systems have been severely damaged by antibiotics can be helped by ingesting fecal matter from healthy individuals. It sounds disgusting, but if you were in danger of losing your life due to a severe and debilitating intestinal infection, my guess is you would get over any squeamishness. A study published in *The New England*

Journal of Medicine in January 2013 reported a 94 percent cure rate of colitis when administering fecal transplants, compared to just 31 percent with the antibiotic vancomycin.[6]

Thomas Louie, a doctor at the University of Calgary, has developed a more palatable treatment in pill form. At present, the pills are customized for individual patients, but someday there may be pills to help some of the half a million Americans a year who get C-diff. Most of us aren't ill enough to need such a radical overhaul of the microorganisms in their GI tract, but nearly everyone shows signs of an imbalanced gut—although we may not link gas, bloating, mood swings, mild depression, and allergies to problems with our digestive flora. When I was in college, I used to think passing gas was just a guy thing, but now I understand that it can happen to anyone when the good bacteria in the gut are compromised by consumption of sugars, processed wheat, and gluten-rich grains.

If we avoid gluten and the cheap carbs in processed wheat, breads, and pasta, and rebuild our flora with good quality probiotics, the digestive system can gradually restore the colonies of friendly microorganisms and eliminate or limit most of the unfriendly ones. But if we continue eating gluten-laden foods, the result is most likely to be inflammation, decreased immunity, and a condition known as leaky gut syndrome.

PERILS OF A LEAKY GUT

The lining of the intestines is only one cell thick, and gluten can loosen the tight junctions in the gut wall. If it becomes permeable, or "leaky," undigested food fragments and bacteria can slip through the gut lining and into the bloodstream. Imagine a net made of stretchy material that becomes more permeable as it stretches. As more foreign bacteria reach the bloodstream, the condition worsens.

In the bloodstream, the immune system treats gluten like an invading bad microbe. This sets off an autoimmune reaction, releasing chemokines and cytokines, the chemical messengers of the immune system, which instruct killer T cells to attack the gut lining. This results not only in digestive disturbances but also in food sensitivities, rashes, joint pain, and inflammation throughout the body. Meanwhile, the liver and kidneys go into overdrive to process all the toxins that have entered the bloodstream, many of which end up passing through the blood-brain barrier.

The effect of leaky gut syndrome on the brain can be dramatic and far-reaching: headaches, brain fog, poor concentration, short-term memory loss. (Many "senior moments" are due to leaky gut.) Some people with leaky gut experience depression or anxiety. Others become hyperactive, impulsive, and short-tempered. The toxic load on the brain disables the higher circuits for love, beauty, creativity, and joy. Worst of all, the brain goes on autopilot, turning the controls over to the more primitive limbic brain, with its four basic responses to life: fight, flee, feed, or fornicate. Through all this, you're struggling to understand why you're so moody, or why you keep misplacing your cell phone, or why your world seems more hostile and threatening. Furthermore, in this condition, you have absolutely no chance of experiencing the higher states of consciousness.

The number one change that can repair a leaky gut and reverse the toxin overload that leads to it is to eliminate sugar and gluten from your diet, and replenish the friendly intestinal flora. Detoxifying from sugar requires eliminating not just the obvious sugary foods but also processed grains, which turn into glucose instantly, spiking your blood sugar. Whole grains contain enough fiber to keep blood-sugar levels steady, but if you want to upgrade your brain to support One Spirit Medicine, you'll need to avoid *all* processed grains. If this seems unnecessarily strict, note that the minimum daily requirement of *processed* carbohydrates is zero.

Eliminating sugar also involves cutting out fruits like watermelon and raisins, which have a higher glycemic index than a Popsicle. Fruits and vegetables that are high in fiber don't have a high glycemic index and they slow the absorption of glucose, so your blood sugar doesn't spike.

FASTING

Central to the process of detoxing is fasting. Abstaining from food has a long history going back millennia as a way to cleanse body and mind in anticipation of spiritual experience. Traditionally, shamans would subsist on water for a few days to prime the brain to function optimally, unmuddled by toxins, in order to receive One Spirit Medicine.

The purpose of fasting is not for weight loss. That's a dangerous misuse of the practice. We fast to turn on the body's repair mechanisms and clear brain fog. Fasting literally brings about cleansing at a cellular level. Reducing the intake of sugars and processed carbs for more than a few hours triggers a process called autophagy, in which debris inside the cells is recycled into a form the cells can use as building blocks.

As cells in the body detox, they eliminate cellular waste into the bloodstream, where it's carried to the gastrointestinal tract and flushed out of the body. When we're consuming sugars the body is in building mode, repairing and creating muscle. When we stop the intake of sugars for a few hours, we go into autophagy and recycling.

Even during a very short fast, amazing things happen to the body and brain. In just 24 hours, the production of human growth hormone increases by 1,500 percent, repairing cells that make up our tissues. Not eating sugars for as little as 18 hours wakes up the body's system for self-repair, detoxifies cells, and switches on the longevity genes. Fasting to detox involves not eating any sugars or grains between 6 P.M. and noon the next day.

FOUR MEALS A DAY

Detoxing through the skin, kidney, liver, and lungs will proceed more efficiently if you eat good, healthy, organic foods during the process. The basic menu to prepare your brain and body for One Spirit awareness consists of plenty of fresh, fibrous vegetables; healthy nuts, seeds, and oils; and omega-3-rich fish. These foods will provide plenty of the right kind of fats to fuel the brain. To support your gut-brain and mitochondrial function, it's advisable to get most of your fats from nuts, seeds, avocados, and healthy oils like coconut oil, cold-pressed extra virgin olive oil, and flaxseed oil.

Also be sure to eat plenty of fibrous cruciferous vegetables like cauliflower, broccoli, and cabbage. The cruciferous vegetables aid in the detox process by switching on the Nrf2 pathway, a genetic pathway that regulates production of antioxidants and detox enzymes, and turns on the longevity genes inside the cells. Avoid root vegetables, which have a high glycemic index, raising blood-sugar levels.

During the detox, limit your fruit intake to one serving a day, eaten in the afternoon, and avoid fruit juices, which will spike your blood sugar. Start your day instead with a fresh green juice made from organic green vegetables. If you wish, you can add a small amount of carrot or apple to the juice to improve the taste.

After your detox, your system will be able to handle moderate amounts of other healthy foods that are not on the detox menu. At that point, you can add one cup of coffee a day and the occasional glass of wine. I'm not suggesting you ban high-glycemic foods like watermelon and beets from your diet for the rest of your life. Just pay attention to your body's signals and your moods so that you will know when you need to detoxify again.

Most of us are used to eating three meals a day, plus snacks. During your seven-day detox, you will eat four meals a day, including two breakfasts, without any junk-food snacks in between!

Upon waking in the morning, begin the day with your first breakfast—a drink made from green, leafy vegetables, particularly kale. Later in the morning, you'll have a second breakfast that will include healthy fats like avocados and proteins like eggs or smoked salmon, but no fruit or grains.

You can have fruit with your lunch if you wish, along with steamed veggies and your choice of protein. The protein might be fish or quinoa, a "pseudo-grain" that is gluten-free and closely related to spinach and beetroot. Nutrient rich, quinoa is high in good fats and protein.

Dinner will be a light meal, again with a protein dish and healthy fats. Just be sure to finish all eating for the day by 6 P.M. This will give you a full 12-hour period of fasting overnight, and 18 hours off the glucose-building system, allowing your cells to go into autophagy.

Although for millennia a plant-based diet was standard fare for humans, most of us aren't used to having green juices, salads, and vegetable soups for breakfast. To make dishes tastier, you can add nuts, seeds, and healthy oils, as well as fresh or dried herbs. While you're preparing for One Spirit Medicine, use only flaxseed oil or extra virgin olive oil to flavor foods and dress salads. For cooking, use only coconut oil, which can withstand high temperatures. Don't cook with olive oil, which breaks down with heat.

Never boil vegetables or overcook them, as you'll break down the fiber and destroy the phytonutrients and vitamins. Instead, steam vegetables or sauté them in vegetable broth with herbs. Or eat them raw, drizzled with healthy oils.

The physical and emotional lift you get from a seven-day detox may inspire you to switch permanently to a plant-based, organic diet with healthy fats and no processed grains. Although reducing your exposure to external poisons will support healthy brain functioning, switching to a diet based on plant nutrients will optimize your body's ability to eliminate toxins and create health.

MENU FOR DETOXING

If you're not sure what to eat during your detox, here are some suggestions for meals and snacks:

- **First Breakfast (7 A.M.):** Green juice. Recipe: 6 small leaves of kale, 2 leaves of collard greens, ½ cucumber, 2 stalks of celery, ½ inch ginger, ½ lemon (peeled), ½ green apple. Drink about 240 ml. No coffee or tea. Drink plenty of water with the meal and throughout the day—a total of 8 glasses at least.

- **Second Breakfast (10 A.M.):** Proteins and fats of your choice. Eggs, goat cheese, avocado, smoked fish, and nuts are all great options.

- **Lunch:** Green salad or a large serving of vegetables steamed or sautéed in vegetable broth. Use healthy oils and herbs and spices for flavor. Combine with a handful of seeds or nuts, an avocado, or a serving of smoked salmon, wild-caught fish, quinoa, or lean, organic, grass-fed meat. Fruit of your choice.

- **Afternoon Snack:** Nuts, seeds, avocado mashed with spices and herbs, a small salad, or green juice.

- **Dinner (finish by 6 P.M.):** Same as lunch.

You can drink green tea throughout the day. Green tea contains minimal caffeine but many antioxidants, and can switch on cellular detox pathways.

DETOXIFYING: WHAT TO EXPECT

For the first few days of detoxification, as you remove sugars, processed grains, and processed foods from your diet, it's normal to feel tired, achy, and uncomfortable. You may also experience gas, bad breath, or headaches while the toxins are leaving your body. Drinking plenty of water will help speed the process by flushing out toxins through the kidneys and bladder. You will also eliminate toxins through the skin: you can expect to sweat more than usual. For the first few days of your detox, allow yourself extra rest. You might want to schedule the start of your detox around a weekend.

Don't be surprised if you experience brain fog and difficulty focusing while you're detoxing. Toxins are stored in the fat in the brain, and during detox your brain will begin to release them into your bloodstream so you can eliminate them.

You may also feel irritable and moody. Physical detox tends to loosen up long-buried emotions. Toxic emotions bind to physical toxins, and your body will be working hard at clearing out the physical and emotional poisons. Pay attention to feelings and memories that surface during this time. You may reexperience old wounds that run deep. Try not to be reactive; this is not the time to make big decisions or confront others about personal issues. Instead, take time to process emotions that are being released.

I recommend journaling during your seven-day detox, so that the people around you won't bear the brunt of any irritability you may feel. Journaling will also help you gain perspective on past experiences that you may be reliving in the present, and processing old hurts may bring you to a place of forgiveness. In fact, after a few days, as your head starts to clear, you're likely to have a very different take on your problems. You may even find that toxic emotions simply evaporate.

Because your body is functioning better, you may find that you're sleeping less but feeling more rested.

MONITORING YOUR PROGRESS

One way to monitor your progress as you're going through detox is to track your fasting glucose levels. You can buy a glucometer for about $10 at a drugstore.

Test your blood sugar in the morning before eating anything. Your glucose level should be between 75 and 90 mg/dl—ideally, below 85. Two hours after you eat, test your glucose level again. It should be no more than 40 points above what it was before you ate. While a fasting glucose of 105 is considered normal, to avoid diabetes and dementia aim for a lower level.

To get an accurate reading of how your glucose levels change as you clean up your diet, test your blood-sugar level daily for a few days before a detox, then during the detox, and then afterward. As you alter your diet to fuel your brain on fats and nutrient-rich plants, test your blood sugar periodically to see how you're making progress on lowering your glucose levels.

Detox will also lower your IGF-1 (insulin-like growth factor) levels. IGF-1 is a protein closely associated with insulin, and a growth factor we need when we are young and are growing fingers and toes. But as adults, high levels of IGF-1 are associated with pathological growth. IGF-1 signals cancer risk—in effect, it's a cancer-tumor marker. As you lower your IGF-1 levels, you reduce your chances of developing cancer and other diseases. When we do blood-chemistry tests on participants in our seven-day Grow a New Body program in Chile, we find that their levels of IGF-1 drop between 30 and 50 percent.

Research cardiologists at the Intermountain Medical Center Heart Institute found that fasting also lowers the risk of coronary artery disease and diabetes, the leading cause of death in America. Even a 24-hour fast will increase the levels of human growth hormone, which repairs the body and maintains metabolic balance, by a staggering 1,300 percent in men and 2,000 percent in women.[7]

BE PATIENT

One of the most important things to remember is that detox is a process. Your limbic brain—the tyrant king—will most likely rebel against your efforts to remove it from its sugar and dopamine-rich throne as the driver of your decisions, emotions, and perceptions. It may insist that nothing's happening, so why bother detoxing? Whatever excuse your primitive brain proffers, don't give in to its insistent voice!

Above all, be patient with yourself during the detox process. Your gut-brain can't repair itself without a little discomfort, and you can't reverse years of bad habits in a few days. But the payoff of even a short detox is that you'll feel far better very quickly—generally within the first three days—and that will prime you to continue a healthier way of living.

SUPPLEMENTS FOR ONE SPIRIT DETOX

Plan to take the following supplements every day during your seven-day detox. You will be taking fairly high doses of some supplements, but only for the duration of the detox. (For more information on the supplements and directions on continuing their use after your detox, see Chapter 5, Superfoods and Super Supplements.)

MORNING (ON ARISING):

Vitamin B12 is essential for liver detoxification and for preserving intact DNA, important for cell growth. Most Americans are B12 deficient. Be sure to take sublingual methylcobalamin, an enhanced form of B12 that dissolves quickly under the tongue. Take 2,500 micrograms (mcg).

Vitamin C is essential for detoxification processes. Take 2,000 milligrams (mg).

Vitamin D3 is essential to enable the body to absorb calcium, and it can prevent or reduce depression, dementia, diabetes, and autoimmune disorders. During the seven-day detox, take 5,000 international units (IU) of vitamin D3.

S-acetyl glutathione is the first truly bioavailable form of the free-radical scavenger glutathione. Take 1 gram in the morning on an empty stomach.

DHA and EPA, docosahexaenoic acid and eicosapentaenoic acid, are omega-3 fatty acids important for brain health and preventing Alzheimer's. They're found in fish, nuts, seeds, and certain oils, but supplements are recommended. Take 3 grams.

Curcumin, the active ingredient in the spice turmeric, activates the genes that turn on powerful antioxidants in the brain. Take 1 gram. Be sure it is in liposomal form.

Trans-resveratrol, found in red wine and red grapes, also triggers production of the brain's antioxidants and regulates genes that activate apoptosis, programmed cell death. Take 500 milligrams (mg).

Pterostilbene, found in blueberries and grapes, works with trans-resveratrol to prevent cancer and other diseases. Take 250 milligrams (mg).

ProAlive Probiotic resettles healthy flora in the gut and facilitates digestion. Take five drops in water. (You can order ProAlive Probiotic at www.ascendedhealth.com.)

Coconut oil is jet fuel for the brain. Take 1 teaspoon in the morning and 1 teaspoon in the midafternoon.

EVENING (TWO HOURS AFTER DINNER):

Alpha-lipoic acid helps eliminate toxins and heavy metals embedded in brain tissue. Take one 600 milligram (mg) capsule.

Magnesium citrate helps with your bowel movement and to eliminate waste, as well as relax your muscles. Take two 500 milligram (mg) capsules or a teaspoonful of powdered.

OTHER AIDS TO DETOXIFICATION

BATHS, BRUSHING, AND SAUNA

The skin is one of the main organs involved in detoxification. You can speed the process of eliminating toxins with detox baths, skin brushing, and saunas or steam baths.

Detox baths work by stimulating the body to release toxins through the skin. You literally sweat them out. Very warm water will cause you to sweat, and Epsom salt, which isn't really salt but magnesium sulfate, can be added to warm bathwater to help with the process. The magnesium is absorbed into your system and loosens toxins, which then are excreted through your pores. Epsom salt also promotes healthy circulation and better utilization of oxygen and minerals, and it can lower blood pressure and reduce inflammation. As an added bonus, Epsom salt will relax your muscles, easing stress.

Adding essential oils to your detox bath will relax you even more. Lavender oil has a scent that has been shown to release muscle tension. Other ingredients you might add to your bath, alone or in combination, are baking soda, apple cider vinegar, and Himalayan salt, all of which can aid in detoxing through the skin.

Remain in the detox bath for about 20 minutes. Be especially careful getting out of the tub so you don't fall. **Saunas** can also enhance the skin's ability to excrete toxins. A conventional sauna, which circulates hot air, causes breathing problems for some people and is not as effective as a far-infrared sauna in aiding detox. Far-infrared rays—*far* refers to the position at the extreme end of the light spectrum— actually penetrate your skin to a depth of about one inch, thereby releasing toxins stored in fat layers under the epidermis.

Steam baths can be somewhat helpful in detoxification. But like a conventional sauna, a steam bath only heats the surface of the skin, so it's not as effective at promoting detox as a far-infrared sauna.

Skin brushing stimulates circulation, which helps with detoxification. Before or during your detox bath, brush the skin all over your body. You can buy a brush for this purpose at a health food store or online. Just be sure to clean the brush regularly and allow it to dry fully between uses. Never share your brush with others.

ADDITIONAL TIPS

Keep your bowels moving once or twice a day. Use a natural herbal laxative if needed, or take **magnesium citrate**, which has a laxative effect.

Limit your intake of meat and eliminate all dairy during your detox.

CHAPTER 5

SUPERFOODS AND SUPER SUPPLEMENTS

Be very, very careful what you put into that head,
because you will never, ever get it out.

—Cardinal Thomas Wolsey, about King Henry VIII

Once you've started eliminating the toxins from your body, the next step is to make sure your diet consists of organic, nutrient-rich, and information-dense foods. Superfoods are foods like blueberries and broccoli, which confer special health benefits. Eating the superfoods and supplements in this chapter can all but eliminate your risk for Alzheimer's, cancer, diabetes, and a host of other diseases of civilization.

Wild versions of many superfoods formed the basis of our earliest ancestors' diet and continue to be central to the diet of many indigenous peoples today. In the few hunter-gatherer societies that still exist, autism, dementia, diabetes, cancer, and autoimmune disorders are very rare or nonexistent. Not coincidentally, the diet in these societies has changed little from the Paleolithic era. Nuts, berries, fruits, vegetables, and small game served as our ancestors' primary food sources long before grain became a dietary staple. Today, most of us live farther away from nature than hunter-gatherers do, and we purchase our food at farmers' markets or grocery stores rather than forage in the wild. But we, too, can come close to the ideal diet if we understand what it includes and why it's so beneficial.

Anthropologists long ago abandoned the idea that meat from hunting big animals was central to the early hunter-gatherer diet. Humans coevolved with the plants, not the animals, and for thousands of years, we were incredibly awkward hunters. (Imagine trying to bring down a large predator with a rock, or drive a herd of buffalo off a cliff to harvest some meat for dinner.) Even after early hunters developed spears 500,000 years ago, animals in the wild could easily outrun them and often outsmart them. Buffalo or mammoth meat was only a rare adjunct to a mostly plant-based diet that included protein sources like nuts, seeds, and insects, and on occasion, fish, small game, or reptiles. When a great beast was captured, it was considered a sacred event, an offering from Spirit to be shared with the village.

Some 50,000 years ago, we became more skilled at the hunt. But even then, animals were considered sacred, and their lives were not to be taken lightly. Before Columbus came to the New World in 1492, there were more than 60 million bison grazing in the Great Plains of North America, but by 1890 there were fewer than 200 left in the United States. Big-game hunters had caused a near extinction; a popular sport of the time was shooting these great creatures from the back of a passenger train crossing the plains and then leaving the carcasses behind to rot on the ground. Indigenous peoples, by contrast, never hunted for sport, and when they killed an animal, they used every bit of it for food, clothing, and sinew.

Starting around 6,000 years ago, the typical human diet changed. Locked into working their fields, agricultural-era humans had a diet centered on the crops they grew. Depending on where they lived, wheat, corn, or rice became their dietary staple. All of these grains are a major source of sugar. Essentially, they were fueling their bodies and brains on glucose.

The wild plants the hunter-gatherers harvested and ate served as both food and medicine. It's only very recently that we've become efficient enough at catching fish and game and breeding animals to make them the centerpiece of our diet. Today, of course, most of the meat and fish on our table isn't free-range or wild, and it's raised under horrific conditions, on a grain-based diet. Even farmed salmon are fed corn. Meanwhile, the meat and fish we buy in the local shops are routinely full of hormones and antibiotics injected into them or added to their feed, raising serious questions about the health of the animal flesh we're consuming.

By now every schoolchild knows the value of green plants in the diet. What most of us don't realize, however, is that plants provide vital information to the body beyond simply ensuring a balanced diet. Scientists have found that plants are master regulators of gene expression in humans. (*Gene expression* refers to the process by which DNA makes the proteins that make up the body.) MicroRNAs—single strands of plant genetic material—actually circulate through the bloodstream, switching genes on and off.[1] These microscopic strands regulate our cholesterol levels and direct the destruction of invading viruses and bacteria. MiRNAs are the ultimate social networkers, sending messages quickly to individual genes. They have the power to switch on the genes that create health and to switch off the genes that create cancer, heart disease, diabetes, and many of the other ailments of civilization.

In over 30 years of clinical research at the University of California Medical Center, physician Dean Ornish, founder and president of the Preventive Medicine Research Institute, has found that a primarily plant-based diet will activate more than 500 disease-preventing genes and deactivate more than 200 disease-causing genes. While Dr. Ornish's program includes whole grains as part of the plant-based diet, I recommend cutting out grains altogether during a seven-day detox, in order to lower your blood sugar to the point of switching on autophagy.

The One Spirit Medicine program relies on juicing green leafy vegetables in the morning, to instruct your genes to repair the organs and systems in your body and restore brain health. The instructions provided by the greens and the supplements will switch on stem cell production in the brain and throughout the body. Most green vegetables have a very low sugar content, so even when you juice them, removing most of the fiber, they won't spike your blood sugar. You can have your fiber-rich veggies later, at lunch. (Fiber slows absorption of sugar and helps digestion, supporting friendly bacteria in the gut.) Be aware: root vegetables like beets and carrots have a high glycemic index and are low in fiber, so they're not recommended during detox.

Some plants are considered superfoods because of their high phytonutrient content and the high quality of the information they provide to your DNA. *Phyto* comes from the Greek for plant; phytonutrients, or phytochemicals, are the naturally occurring compounds in plants that protect them from bad bacteria, fungi, pests, and other invaders, and account for their antioxidant, anti-inflammatory, and other healing properties. Phytonutrients are the reason the tribes I met along the Amazon did not suffer from the four greatest maladies of modern life: cancer, heart disease, diabetes, and dementia.

Phytonutrient-rich plants like the cruciferous vegetables, tomatoes, and various nuts and seeds are central to the diets of people who live in blue zones—areas around the globe where the inhabitants have unusually high longevity and good health, most notably Okinawa, Japan; Sardinia, Italy; Nicoya, Costa Rica; Ikaria, Greece; and Loma Linda, California, which is home to a large community of Seventh-Day Adventists, a religious group that maintains a lacto-ovo vegetarian diet.

As a rule of thumb, the more colorful a fruit or vegetable is, the richer it is in phytonutrients and the greater its power as a superfood. While we can also ingest phytonutrients in the form of nutritional supplements, eating them in their natural form is preferable, to get the full benefits of their living nutrients.

No matter how carefully we think we're eating, we may still be missing out on phytonutrients, however. Research indicates that much of the produce found in supermarkets is relatively deficient in phytonutrients compared to produce sold at farm stands and farmers' markets or picked from your kitchen garden. And even farm-fresh produce can't match the power of its wilder cousins. As Jo Robinson, author of *Eating on the Wild Side: The Missing Link to Optimum Health,* explains, "Wild dandelions, once a springtime treat for Native Americans, have seven times more phytonutrients than spinach, which we consider a 'superfood.' A purple potato native to Peru has 28 times more cancer-fighting anthocyanins [flavonoids] than common russet potatoes. One species of apple has a staggering 100 times more phytonutrients than the Golden Delicious displayed in our supermarkets."[2]

The reason for this nutrient loss, Robinson explains, is that for the last 10,000 years, farmers have been selecting the sweetest, least bitter plants to grow in their fields, selectively breeding out the sour taste of most wild foods. Today we understand that the bitter, astringent flavor of some vegetables indicates that the plant is high in polyphenols that protect it from disease and pests. But our farming ancestors selected plants that were high in sugar and low in fiber—quick energy sources that were tastier to eat. The result was a steady decline in health benefits.

For maximum benefit, we should eat vegetables and fruits that are in season, free of pesticides, and locally grown. The fruits and vegetables that most grocery stores sell as fresh are picked days or weeks before they're ripe, with the idea that they'll ripen in transit. But in the process, they lose much of the flavor and nutritional value they would have gained from ripening naturally under the sun. Supporting local farmers not only ensures that our produce will be fresh but also reduces the carbon footprint of transporting foods long distances. If good, fresh fruits and vegetables aren't available locally, the best alternative is frozen organic produce; frozen fruits and vegetables are picked at the height of freshness and immediately flash-frozen. Canned fruits and vegetables should be avoided at all costs; processed foods contain all sorts of chemicals and other unhealthy additives, and much of the nutritional value has been lost. Whenever the opportunity to gather wild foods presents itself, go for it. Nothing tastes quite like a salad of wild dandelion greens!

CRUCIFEROUS VEGETABLES

Among the healthiest of the superfoods are the cruciferous vegetables, which include broccoli, cauliflower, cabbage, and kale. (*Cruciferous* doesn't refer to a property of the vegetables but rather to the petals of the plants, which grow in the shape of a cross.) High in fiber and antioxidants as well as phytonutrients, cruciferous vegetables activate the Nrf2 detox system inside cells and turn on the longevity genes.

Nrf2 is a powerful protein and transcription factor able to protect every organ in the body and every kind of tissue against diseases like cancer, heart disease, dementia, lung injury, and autoimmune disease. It is one of the most important cellular defense mechanisms designed to cope with oxidants—free radicals—and oxidative stress produced by toxins and carcinogens. (A free radical is a molecule that has lost an electron and tries to steal one from another molecule, leading to inflammation and a host of other medical challenges.)

Broccoli originated in the Mediterranean and is mentioned in ancient Roman texts. Commonly used in Italian cooking, it first came to America when Thomas Jefferson brought it from Europe. Broccoli is usually green, but there's a purple variety as well. Both the stems and florets are edible. Broccoli can be steamed, baked, roasted, grilled, or chopped up and eaten raw in a salad. It can also be used in a soup or casserole, although you'll want to avoid thick, creamy soups and cheesy casseroles, which contain dairy and bad fats. Broccoli is rich in calcium, selenium, and zinc, among other nutrients. Broccoli is also high in sulforaphane, a powerful antioxidant that switches on cellular detoxification pathways. It shows anticancer properties and upregulates the expression of the longevity genes inside cells.

Cauliflower originated in both Europe and Asia. It is usually white, but there are also purple and orange varieties. Packed with nutrients and high in fiber, cauliflower is often used in Indian curries and roasted with the spice turmeric, another phytonutrient. Like broccoli, cauliflower can be steamed, baked, grilled, or eaten raw, and can be used in a soup or casserole.

Cabbage and **Brussels sprouts**, recognizable by their heads of tightly packed leaves, are loaded with nutrients. In fact, cabbage was used in ancient Greece and Rome to remedy myriad illnesses. Brussels sprouts are rich in folic acid and vitamins A and C, but if undercooked they have a bitter taste that makes them the least favorite vegetables in the cruciferous family. That's too bad, as grilled or baked, they are very tasty.

Bok choy, or white cabbage, is a staple of Asian cooking. Cultivated in China for over 6,000 years, it is now grown in North America as well. Nutrient dense, bok choy contains a whopping 28 phytochemicals,[3] including one found to prevent ovarian cancer,[4] and it's high in vitamins A, C, and K, foliate, and the mineral calcium. Bok choy is a good source of calcium, as unlike spinach it is low in oxalate, a substance that binds to calcium and makes it unavailable to the body. Bok choy can be eaten cooked or raw, and is a healthy addition to a green juice.

Kale, like spinach and other greens that don't form a head, has become wildly popular in the West—deservedly so. It's packed with fiber and phytonutrients, and is a good source of vitamins C, K, and beta-carotene, as well as calcium and magnesium. I drink kale every morning in my green juice, as it is one of the most potent and vibrant plants. The bluer the color, the more nutritious it is.

Collard greens have a phytonutrient content that's off the charts. Research shows they may be the most effective of the cruciferous vegetables at lowering cholesterol, and they reduce the risk of cancer and cardiovascular disease. Among the oldest members of the cabbage family, collard greens were popular in ancient Greece and Rome. They came to America from Africa with the slave trade and are such an integral part of traditional Southern cooking that South Carolina declared collard greens the state vegetable. They can be cooked in a variety of ways, and their wide leaves can be used like bread or tortillas as a wrap for other vegetables.

Mustard greens, which can be red as well as green, have a peppery taste resembling arugula's. Phytonutrient superstars, mustard greens are right behind collard greens and kale in cholesterol-lowering ability, and among the crucifers, they are second only to Brussels sprouts in cancer prevention. For maximum nutritional benefit, chop the greens, then let them sit for five minutes before cooking.

Celery was cultivated by the Romans and has been found in Egyptian tombs. It was even used ceremonially in the Arctic Circle and Alaska, where hardy varieties grow. North Americans eat the stalk of Pascal celery, the variety most commonly grown here, while in Europe, the dominant variety is celeriac, in which the leaves and bulb are eaten but not the stalk. Celery contains vitamins, notably K, and trace minerals like calcium, and is a good source of fiber. Paired with nut butter, it makes a healthy and delicious snack. But be warned: like nuts and shellfish, celery can cause a severe immune system reaction, even anaphylactic shock, in someone allergic to it.

CRUCIFEROUS VEGETABLES		
bok choy	cabbage	collard greens
broccoli	cauliflower	kale
Brussels sprouts	celery	mustard greens

OTHER PHYTONUTRIENT-RICH VEGETABLES

Arugula, known as "rocket" in Europe, is a leafy green with a spicy taste. It contains antioxidants and phytonutrients that boost the immune system and is rich in vitamins A, C, and K. Arugula is a popular salad green, but those who find the taste too peppery can mix it with other, milder greens or use baby arugula, which is less pungent. Arugula pesto makes a tasty spread for grilled vegetables or shrimp: pulse the leaves in a food processor with olive oil and crushed walnuts—another superfood—or pine nuts.

Spinach is loaded with magnesium, beta-carotene, and vitamin C, and is even a source of omega-3 fatty acids. Like tomatoes and Brussels sprouts, spinach supplies alpha-lipoic acid, which is important for the synthesis of glutathione, an antioxidant crucial to brain function.

Swiss chard is one of the most nutritious vegetables. It is easily identified by its red stalks and veins, which contain pigments called betalains that provide important antioxidant, anti-inflammatory, and detoxification support. Chard leaves also contain syringic acid, a flavonoid found to control blood sugar.

Lettuces are excellent phytonutrients for salads. For maximum nutrition, choose darker, loose-leafed varieties. Just about any vegetables, cooked or raw, can be tossed into a salad with lettuce. You can dress it with oil, vinegar, lemon, and herbs but avoid creamy dressings and commercial dressings, which usually contain sugars and preservatives.

Kelp, a form of seaweed popular in Asia, particularly in Japanese cooking, is high in calcium and an excellent source of vitamins C and K, riboflavin, and folic acid. But be warned, it's also high in sodium.

Parsley is the world's most popular herb. Though frequently used as a garnish, it's far more than merely decorative. Vitamin-rich parsley contains a whopping 533 percent of our daily requirement of vitamin K and is a good source of vitamin C. Parsley's cancer-fighting ability is a lesser-known attribute: it contains oils that inhibit tumor growth in the lungs, and properties that neutralize carcinogens in smoke from cigarettes and charcoal-grill fires.

Cilantro, also known as Chinese parsley, is a favorite herb in Mexican cuisine. It contains compounds that bind to toxic metals, so it's a good herb to include in a detox diet. Cilantro is thought to promote digestive health, and a tea brewed from the leaves can help settle an upset stomach.

Basil is another herb with healing properties that's a favorite among cooks—it's the main ingredient in a classic pesto and pairs nicely with other superfoods, particularly tomatoes. Like **thyme**, basil contains oils with antibacterial properties, and it may help reduce bad bacteria in the gut. Basil is also rich in magnesium, which promotes heart health.

TURMERIC

Along with all the healthy veggies that are central to the One Spirit Medicine diet is **turmeric**, a spice loaded with health benefits. A key ingredient in curry, turmeric is important for detoxification and brain repair, and is an extremely powerful anti-inflammatory, antioxidant, antifungal, and antimicrobial. In India, where turmeric is a staple of the diet, the rate of Alzheimer's disease is less than a quarter of what it is in the U.S. Turmeric's health benefits are optimized when it's cooked, but it can also be combined with black pepper and taken as a food supplement.

Derived from the root of the *Curcuma longa* plant, turmeric is said to enhance sexual desire and was traditionally used in marriage rituals in India and Tamil. The Sanskrit for turmeric is *haridra*. Haridra Ganesha is one of the 32 aspects of Lord Ganesha, the elephant-headed Hindu god who purifies devotees and brings them luck. Turmeric continues to play a role in rituals throughout Asia, where it's associated with good fortune, abundance, prosperity, and health.

Turmeric has an earthy, strong flavor and, when dried, a deep yellow-orange color that suggests a connection to the life-giving power of the sun.

Curcumin is the active ingredient in turmeric, and its powers include cancer prevention, reduction of free radicals, and support for the heart, liver, and gastrointestinal system. Curcumin also helps lower cholesterol. Known to treat infections and to reduce harmful flora in the gut and on the skin, curcumin activates the genes that turn on BDNF (brain-derived neurotrophic factor) and glutathione, powerful antioxidants produced by the brain. It also activates the SIRT1 gene, the so-called longevity gene. When curcumin is taken as a supplement, the standard dose is one gram per day. Unfortunately, curcumin has very poor bioavailability, that is, very little of what you ingest actually gets into your system. The best form of curcumin is in liposomal (fat based) form, as nanoparticles.

NUTS AND SEEDS

Nuts and seeds are excellent sources of healthy, plant-based fats. Oils from coconuts, walnuts, almonds, and flaxseeds are, like extra virgin olive oil, concentrated sources of omega-3 fatty acids and confer a long list of health benefits, from lowering cholesterol to lifting depression.

Among **nuts**, walnuts are phytonutrient superstars, but other varieties also have significant talents. Almonds are high in fiber. Brazil nuts contain selenium, a cancer fighter. Cashews are rich in iron, zinc, and magnesium, a brain booster. Pecans help prevent plaque from forming on the arteries. Macadamia nuts contain the most monounsaturated (good) fat of any nut, helping lower cholesterol. Peanuts—technically legumes, not nuts—are packed with nutrients, but it's best to avoid them. Many people are sensitive to peanuts, and full-blown peanut allergies are common—and can be fatal.

Seeds are another good way to up your protein and omega-3 intake. Hemp seeds, with ten essential amino acids, are an excellent protein source, and they contain omega-3 and omega-6 fatty acids in an ideal ratio. Sesame seeds are high in calcium and other minerals. Sunflower seeds promote healthy digestion. Pumpkin seeds contain cholesterol-lowering lignans and aid digestion by regulating the passage of food from the stomach to the small intestine.

Both nuts and seeds can be sprinkled on salads, included in vegetable dishes, or eaten plain. To get the most nutritional value out of nuts and seeds, be sure to buy unroasted organic ones and store them in the refrigerator to keep them fresh and prevent mold.

AVOCADOS

The ancient peoples of the Americas knew that the fruit of the avocado tree was a superfood offering a host of benefits. Don't be put off by the high fat content; avocados contain healthy mono-unsaturated fats including oleic acid, which lowers the risk of breast cancer and increases nutrient absorption in the gut. Avocados are a good source of lutein, a carotenoid that prevents macular degeneration, and of folic acid, a B vitamin that prevents heart disease and strokes. High in fiber with a low glycemic index, avocados help regulate blood sugar. They're also a good source of the antioxidant glutathione, and when paired with spinach or tomatoes, which are high in alpha-lipoic acid, they pack a one-two punch that protects cell health. Guacamole, made with avocados, tomatoes, parsley, and a little lime, salt, and onion, makes a phytonutrient-rich dip. Just don't grab a bag of tortilla chips for dipping; cut up some raw vegetables instead.

BERRIES

Blueberries are phytonutrient rock stars, containing pterostilbene, which lowers cholesterol and blood pressure, and protects against cancer and dementia. Among the few fruits native to North America, blueberries were a dietary staple of Native American tribes across the northeastern U.S. Known for their antioxidant properties, blueberries are also rich in iron, selenium, and zinc. If you can find the wild variety, grab them; their nutrient value is even higher.

Goji berries, also known as wolfberries, are native to China, where they've been touted for centuries as the key to long life. Nutrient dense, the berries contain two to four times the antioxidant properties of blueberries as well as all nine essential amino acids, making them a whole protein source, like meat. The goji berry is a staple of traditional Chinese medicine. Though goji berries are generally eaten raw or brewed in a tea or cooked in soup, for medicinal purposes, extracts are commonly used.

WHAT TO EAT IN MODERATION

Ancient humans didn't have access to fruit year-round, so their bodies adjusted to eating only the fruits that grew where they lived, harvested in season. Except in tropical climates, *in season* meant when the fruit ripened at the end of the growing season— the end of summer. From an evolutionary standpoint, the role of insulin—the hormone produced by the pancreas to signal cells to absorb sugar—was to turn fruit sugars into fat that was stored by the body to provide energy for our hunter-gatherer ancestors throughout the long winter. Today, however, the long winter with few food sources never arrives, so we're stuck with excess fat, typically in the midsection. Since our bodies haven't evolved to eat fruit in large quantities after the growing season, consuming too much of it throws off the insulin system, causing blood sugar to spike, sometimes dangerously so. Therefore, we should eat only a moderate amount of fruit, consuming it as whole fruit, not juice, to prevent blood-sugar spikes and get the full benefit of the fiber. If fruit is out of season, but you *really* crave it, try eating a few frozen blueberries or sprinkle a small amount of dried fruit—berries, grapes, or cherries—onto a salad.

The exception to the no-juice rule is the green drink to start off the day. Avoid premixed green drinks sold commercially; most are just fruit juice with a little kale or spinach added to color them green. Making your own juice with fresh leafy green vegetables will give you a lasting infusion of vitamins and micronutrients, including those that turn off the genes for disease and turn on the genes for health. Until you get used to the bitterness of green juice, you may find it more palatable if you blend in a small amount of fresh or frozen berries.

During a detox, avocados, nuts, seeds, and eggs (unless you're allergic to them) are good sources of protein while you prepare for the vision quest. You should avoid red meat while detoxing, but after that, as you start to upgrade your gut-brain, you can eat red meat in moderation. Fish and red meat are "full" or "complete" proteins, meaning they contain all nine essential amino acids.

Don't eat just any meat, however. Find the cleanest free-range meat and poultry you can; food animals allowed to graze with other animals and consume a natural, plant-based diet are high in omega-3 fatty acids. Limit red-meat intake to once a week. (I personally have eliminated all red meat from my diet, with no adverse effect on my health.)

As for fish, if it's not a part of your diet, it should be—even if all that's available to you is the canned variety. When our ancestors left the African savannah for the coast, they incorporated fish and mollusks into their diet. All over the world, civilizations sprang up around oceans, lakes, and rivers. Emperors, governors, and high priests dined on shellfish, mollusks, and fish, while their pyramid-building subjects were fed wheat and bread. But today fish is within the reach of most everyone who lives near seafood-rich waters or can open a tin of sardines.

Packed with the omega-3 essential fatty acid DHA, fish is superior brain food that prepares us for the experience of One Spirit Medicine. Avoid farmed fish, which are often pumped full of antibiotics and supplements to enhance color, and fed soybeans and grain that they would never eat in the wild. The wild varieties—especially cold-water fish like Alaskan wild salmon, sardines, and herring—are lower in toxins. But bear in mind that the larger the fish, the more likely it is to be contaminated with mercury, so avoid tuna and swordfish.

It's interesting to note that the DHA-rich fish oil was so highly prized by North American Indians from the Pacific Northwest that it was traded like currency. The "grease" (or extract) produced from the so-called candlefish was so rich in oil that you could simply stick a wick in the mouth of one of the dried fish, and it would burn like a candle!

FERMENTED FOODS

Fermentation is an ancient method of food preparation going back to at least 8000 B.C.E., and you can find fermented foods in every part of the world. Based on culturing friendly bacteria, fermentation produces everything from wine, beer, and cider to bread, cheese, and vinegar. Fermented foods provide essential enzymes and probiotics that repair the gut and help rid the body of toxins, including heavy metals.

My favorite fermented foods are pickles, sauerkraut, and miso soup. You can find excellent recipes for fermented foods on the Internet, as well as how-to videos on the culturing process. If you're going to ferment foods yourself, just make sure to follow the directions carefully, to avoid contamination from unwanted bacteria.

For our ancestors, fermentation was a way of preserving food and maximizing its health benefits, using naturally occurring bacteria to convert sugars into lactic acid. Sally Fallon and Mary G. Enig, Ph.D., of the Weston A. Price Foundation, which disseminates research and information on nutrient-dense foods, explain how fermentation works:

> Starches and sugars in vegetables and fruits are converted into lactic acid by the many species of lactic-acid-producing bacteria. These lactobacilli are

ubiquitous, present on the surface of all living things and especially numerous on leaves and roots of plants growing in or near the ground. Man needs only to learn the techniques for controlling and encouraging their proliferation to put them to his own use, just as he has learned to put certain yeasts to use in converting the sugars in grape juice to alcohol in wine.[5]

ANTIBIOTICS, PREBIOTICS, AND PROBIOTICS

Americans have been overusing antibiotics for decades. Antibiotics wreak havoc with your microbiome, yet it's increasingly difficult to find meat or poultry or dairy that hasn't been tainted with antibiotics. Pigs, chickens, and cattle are routinely given antibiotic-laced feed to keep them healthy while they're confined in crowded pens, and the antibiotics end up on our dinner tables.

Prebiotics and probiotics are essential for upgrading your gut-brain. They can help reverse the effects of antibiotic use as well as prevent further damage.

Prebiotics promote the growth of good flora in your gut. Cruciferous vegetables have been called prebiotics because they contain fiber that the good flora feed on, serving as the latticework for growing good flora. To upgrade your brain and keep it functioning optimally, you need to consume plenty of plant fiber, or roughage. Fiber speeds the movement of food through the digestive system by absorbing water, which softens stools, making defecation easier.

Probiotics are the healthy flora that facilitate digestion and protect the gut against harmful microbes. We take in some probiotics in our ordinary interactions with the natural environment, whether it's by inhaling dust that rises from the soil as we garden, or by petting a dog or cat, or simply by holding another person's hand. In fact, there are myriad ways we bring healthy organisms into the body, ranging from handling organic fruits and vegetables before rinsing off the soil to swimming in a lake or stream. A single gram of earth—about the size of a small coin—contains over 40 billion probiotic bacteria. As part of upgrading your gut-brain for One Spirit Medicine, I recommend spending more time outdoors!

If you don't feel you're getting enough probiotics in the ordinary course of your life, you can take a supplement. The best I've found are the "smart" probiotics that my friend Compton Rom Bada, a microbiologist, has gathered from the five longevity regions around the planet. (You can order his ProAlive Probiotic at ascendedhealth.com.) Compton's bio-intelligent probiotics can repopulate the flora in your gut in a matter of weeks, whereas off-the-shelf formulas that contain dead or inactive flora generally take much longer and aren't as effective.

NUTRITIONAL SUPPLEMENTS

Changing your eating habits is an essential part of receiving One Spirit Medicine and sustaining its benefits. But it can be challenging to follow all the dietary recommendations, especially at the times of the year when farm-fresh, locally grown produce isn't available in your area. Nutritional supplements can help you get on the fast track to detoxing, as well as repair your gut and maintain a brain-friendly diet.

We have spoken about many of these supplements in the previous chapter, but only in the context of the seven-day detox program. Here we will review them in the role they can have in your everyday diet. These supplements affect the gut-brain in different ways, but they all play a role in how your brain and the organs in your body repair and regenerate. Be sure to check with your health-care professional before taking any supplements, and listen to your body. There's a right dosage for each person, and it's slightly different for everyone, even during different seasons. Pay close attention to how you feel, and learn your body's subtle messages.

DHA, docosahexaenoic acid, is an omega-3 fatty acid that is extremely important for brain health; in fact, it makes up 40 percent of the brain. Breast milk is nearly 50 percent DHA. DHA works closely with another omega-3 fatty acid, **EPA**, eicosapentaenoic acid. Both are found in fish, nuts, seeds, and certain oils. Since the body doesn't make DHA-EPA, it's recommended that you take three grams daily as fish oil or an algae derivative. The best DHA comes from krill. Researchers have noted an 85 percent reduction in the risk for Alzheimer's among people with high levels of DHA in their diet.[6]

ALA, alpha-lipoic acid, is found in every cell in the body and plays an important role in detoxification. ALA can cross the blood-brain barrier, so it helps release toxins from the brain. In a process known as chelation, ALA binds to heavy metals so they can be excreted through the liver, kidneys, and skin. ALA also supports the liver's ability to eliminate toxins during detoxification. You can take 300 milligrams (mg) a day.

Turmeric, a spice identified as a superfood, increases levels of SOD, or superoxide dismutase, and glutathione—two antioxidants important to brain functioning that are described in detail in Chapter 6, Resetting the Death Clock. The dosage is one gram a day of curcumin, the active ingredient in turmeric, in tablet form, or half of this amount if taken in a liposomal form.

Trans-resveratrol, a compound found in red wine, red grape skins, and certain berries, turns on longevity genes and triggers the production of antioxidants. Resveratrol also boosts SOD and glutathione, the brain's super antioxidants. The recommended dose is 500 mg a day.

Pterostilbene, found in blueberries and grapes, has been shown to lower cholesterol and glucose, and reduce blood pressure. Working together, pterostilbene and trans-resveratrol prevent cancer, heart disease, diabetes, and other illnesses. Trans-resveratrol works upstream, regulating the genes that activate apoptosis—programmed cell death, or cell suicide—while pterostilbene works downstream, turning off the genes that allow cancer cells to grow and proliferate. One 250 mg capsule of pterostilbene a day is recommended.

Vitamin B12 is essential for liver detoxification and for repairing the myelin sheath around neurons. It is also needed for preserving the integrity of DNA for cell reproduction and for production of neurotransmitters. Most Americans are B12 deficient. Take 2,000 micrograms (mcg) a week of sublingual methylcobalamin B12—a more bioavailable form. During the seven-day detox, I recommend a dose of 2,500 mcg daily for the week.

Vitamin C is essential for all detoxification processes. Take one gram daily.

Vitamin D3 is the form of vitamin D that the body manufactures when it's exposed to sunlight. But even if you spend a great deal of time outdoors, it's unlikely you're getting enough vitamin D3. Fish and fish liver oils are almost the only dietary sources of vitamin D, although egg yolks, beef liver, fortified milk, and cheese contain small amounts. Vitamin D deficiency has been linked to seasonal depression, diabetes, dementia, and autoimmune disorders. Individuals who take 600 international units (IU) or more of vitamin D3 show 50 percent less dementia and Alzheimer's than control groups.[7] Dosage varies widely, but in a review of current research, vitamin D expert Michael Holick, M.D., cites therapeutic doses for adults ranging from 800 to 1,000 IU a day to 10,000 IU a day, for a maximum of five months.[8]

S-acetyl glutathione (A-GSH) is the first truly bioavailable form of glutathione, which scavenges free radicals. It protects DNA from damage and is crucial for energy metabolism and optimal mitochondrial function.[9] It also supports detoxification of the liver, lungs, kidneys, and other organs.[10] Take 200 mg daily.

Coconut oil, while not a nutritional supplement, is jet fuel for the brain. It is a medium-chain triglyceride, which means it goes through the intestinal wall without causing an insulin spike and into the mitochondria inside cells. Take two tablespoons daily—one tablespoon in the morning and one tablespoon midafternoon or at night. You can also add coconut oil to soup and tea.

Nutritional supplements are powerful medicines, and should be used with caution. We are already taking too many vitamins and minerals that are poorly absorbed by the gut. See the guide on page 55 (Chapter 4, Detoxifying the Gut-Brain) for using supplements to support your body to detox naturally.

PART III

OVERCOMING THE DEATH THAT STALKS YOU

CHAPTER 6

RESETTING THE DEATH CLOCK

There is no greater mistake than
to try to leap an abyss in two jumps.

—David Lloyd George, British prime minister

Biology programmed us for reproduction, not for longevity. Mother Nature wants us to procreate so humanity will not be threatened with extinction. So, while immortality belongs to the species, death claims the individual. At around age 35, certain systems in the body begin to decline. We stop producing growth hormone, which builds muscle and keeps skin youthful and elastic, and free-radical scavengers. Wrinkles begin to appear, we do not heal as quickly as we once did, and our notion of a late night out means being in bed by 11 P.M.

Selecting for short-term survival—sometimes to the point of compromising our health in later years—the body performs a kind of triage, explains Bruce Ames, Ph.D., director of the Center for Nutrition and Metabolism at Children's Hospital Oakland Research Institute in Oakland, California. Vitamins and minerals are used first by the proteins needed for immediate survival and reproduction, at the expense of longevity proteins like SIRT1 that defend against the diseases of aging and are essential for long-term health. As a result, a large percentage of the world's population, including people in the U.S. and Europe, are deficient in one or more essential vitamins and minerals. Among the poor, the deficiency is largely due to malnutrition, and among the affluent, to malabsorption of nutrients by a damaged gut. The liver normally stores a few years' worth of vitamin B12, but if you are not able to absorb B12 from your food, you will be deficient in this essential vitamin.

Indigenous peoples understand the universal adage that youth is wasted on the young. They prize the wisdom of age as much as adolescent beauty and feats of strength and endurance. They honor their elders for the guidance they offer. For the indigenous, knowledge is held not in books but in the collective memory of the elders. In the same way we protect our university libraries, indigenous peoples protect their living repositories of knowledge. Without being able to explain biochemistry, Amazon shamans found ways to switch on the longevity proteins and repair longevity genes damaged by stress and short-term survival needs. They discovered the plants that remove toxins and debris from inside the cells and repair the mitochondria, the power centers that convert energy from food into a form cells can use. Switching on the longevity system begins with repairing the mitochondria.

Our Paleolithic ancestors didn't have a clue, of course, what mitochondria were. They simply referred to whatever prevented aging and decline as "the feminine life force." Today, science offers a less mystical explanation of this life force.

Mitochondria are tiny threadlike organelles in the cells that convert carbohydrates into energy in the process known as metabolism. There are competing theories of how they came to be the power plants of human cells. One version holds that mitochondria evolved from the first oxygen-breathing organisms on earth. Billions of years ago, primitive bacteria fed on each other and on the abundant chemicals in the primordial soup of the earth's oceans. As food supplies became scarce, the first blue-green algae appeared and discovered a new food source, the sun, and a way of turning sunlight into fuel. This was a monumental breakthrough—the process we know as photosynthesis. With that, there was abundant food for any organisms that could feed directly on sunlight. But green life also produced as a by-product a highly poisonous gas: oxygen. Most of the free oxygen in the atmosphere was absorbed by the rocks, but once they were saturated, oxygen levels in the atmosphere built up with increasing speed. Since most life forms at that time did not breathe oxygen, this caused a global extinction event. There was an exception: mitochondria, the first oxygen breathers, who became the most successful life form on earth.

As multicelled organisms evolved, mitochondria insinuated themselves into the bodies of plants and animals, enjoying a harmonious symbiotic relationship with the cells of their hosts until finally the mitochondria actually moved *inside* the cells. In exchange for a warm, safe environment, they supplied fuel to the cells.

Mitochondria have their own DNA, separate from ours, and while the structure of our DNA is a double helix, theirs resembles a string of pearls. We have more than 24,000 genes; mitochondria have only 38. But oh, how important those 38 genes are! Not only are mitochondria the body's fuel factories, metabolizing oxygen to produce the fuel for life, but they are also the keepers of the body's death clock, controlling the process of cell suicide, or programmed cell death, known as apoptosis. When the death clock is running properly, old cells know exactly when they need to die to be replaced by healthy new ones. But when the death clock is off, cells don't know they need to die, and the result is cancer. Or they die off too quickly, and the result is accelerated aging.

THE FUEL OF LIFE

Mitochondrial DNA is handed down through the mother's genes. So mitochondria quite literally represent the feminine life force recognized by the ancients, passed from generation to generation. Just as millions of years ago cells thrived as the result of collaborating with mitochondria, human bodies today can thrive if we repair and nurture this feminine force. Mitochondria not only hold the key to our health but also provide the fuel we need to access the higher neural networks that help us experience One Spirit Medicine.

That fuel is ATP, adenosine triphosphate. ATP is the body's currency: the cells spend what they need and deposit the rest in the bank, the liver, where it is stored until needed to power various body functions.

To produce ATP, mitochondria combust oxygen, in much the way your automobile engine burns oxygen to release the energy in gasoline, though in a far less explosive fashion. As we inhale oxygen, it is transported through the bloodstream to the mitochondria in cells throughout the body, where they convert energy from the food we eat into ATP.

Without healthy, high-functioning mitochondria, every cell is at risk. Some 200 ailments we suffer from today—from cancer, heart disease, fibromyalgia, and chronic fatigue to Parkinson's disease, dementia, cirrhosis, and migraine headaches—have been linked to mitochondrial breakdown. Mitochondria are easily damaged by toxins, including pharmaceuticals. Reviewing current research, naturopath John Neustadt and psychiatrist Steve Pieczenik found that "medications have now emerged as a major cause of mitochondrial damage, which may explain many adverse effects. All classes of psychotropic drugs have been documented to damage mitochondria, as have statin medications, analgesics such as acetaminophen, and many others."[1]

Damaged mitochondria reproduce more quickly than healthy ones and feed only on sugars, unlike healthy mitochondria, which are also able to feed on fats. Because cancer cells, with their deficient mitochondria, feed on sugars, scientists see reducing or eliminating dietary carbs as an effective means of fighting and preventing cancer.[2]

When mitochondria are damaged, your metabolism slows. Your body no longer remembers how to burn fat, and you can't lose weight. The fat stores in your body become repositories for toxins. You're likely to feel moody, fatigued, and generally unwell. With big dips in energy, you're more likely to reach for a quick fix like a power bar, which only exacerbates the problem by feeding the sugar-hungry bacteria in your gut and raising your blood-sugar levels. Inflammation results, oxidative stress worsens, and more mitochondria are damaged. As programmed cell death stops working properly, defective mitochondria accumulate inside the cells, accelerating aging. Damaged cells grow uncontrollably, forming tumors. Brain cells begin to age or die off, damaging regions of the brain. When the apoptosis death clock isn't functioning properly, you compromise your health span and shorten your life span.

AUTOPHAGY, OR RECYCLING MITOCHONDRIA

Eliminating ailing mitochondria and supporting the birth of vibrant, potent mitochondria is crucial for brain repair. Autophagy, Greek for "self-eating," is the garbage collection service inside the cells, the process by which cellular waste is broken down, and dead and damaged mitochondria are recycled to harvest amino acids, the building blocks of new cells.

Aerobic exercise triggers autophagy; exercise consumes oxygen, which kills off weak mitochondria while fostering the growth of more vigorous replacements. Detoxifying is another way to jump-start mitochondria recycling. And eating a diet high in phytonutrients switches on the antioxidant machinery inside the cells that repairs mitochondria.

The most effective and painless way of supporting autophagy is through fasting. Even a short fast between dinner and breakfast the next day causes the body to go into repair mode. Fasting puts the body into ketosis—the mitochondria switch from feeding on glucose to feeding on stored fats. We evolved to store fat we could later consume; our ancestors had to eat when they could and then fast until the next lucky catch of fish or the seasonal harvest of fruit. The body's ability to switch over to burning fat gave us an edge when it came to surviving harsh winters when food was scarce. But the mitochondria can't make the switch if we continually eat grains and sugars, which keep the insulin system turned on. We have to shut down the insulin system so the mitochondria in the brain can switch their fuel source to fats. When the body switches from being a carb-burning machine to a fat-burning one, brain fog lifts and you can lose weight.

Consuming healthy fats like avocados, coconut oil, and olive oil fuels the brain and the heart in the form of ketone bodies— molecules the liver produces from fatty acids when we have to burn fat instead of glucose. Ketones are many times more efficient a fuel than sugars.[3] But as soon as you eat carbs and the insulin system kicks in, the mitochondria treat the sugar as the first course, filling up and forgetting about the rest of the meal. Any extra sugar has to go somewhere, so your pancreas produces insulin to transport it to cells that can use it. But if the cells already have plenty of glucose, they'll refuse the delivery, just as if they were pushing away a dessert plate. Since there's no point in letting that delicious chocolate cake go to waste, your body will make sure the glucose is stored as fat. Since you're no longer able to turn off the insulin system and turn on the fat-burning engines, waste and debris accumulate inside your cells, wreaking havoc on your mitochondria.

Once high blood sugar becomes chronic, you have a prediabetic condition. Unable to absorb more sugar, your cells reduce the number of receptors for insulin in their membranes, resulting in insulin resistance. But the pancreas, registering a buildup of sugar levels in your blood, continues to pump out more insulin. Finally, inflammation and cellular damage occur.

If you're consuming large amounts of carbs, gaining weight around your belly, and experiencing mood swings and brain fog associated with blood-sugar fluctuations, you're already on your way toward insulin resistance and mitochondrial damage. By reducing sugars and grains in your diet and changing to a ketogenic diet—one high in plant foods and healthy fats, and low in carbs—you will stop pressuring the pancreas to go into overdrive and thereby quiet the insulin system. Autophagy will kick in. Toxins stored in the cells can be excreted. Dead mitochondria can be recycled for their reusable building blocks. The system runs as it's supposed to.

When the system goes awry, it behaves like a city where the garbage collectors are on strike. First, garbage accumulates in the kitchen, then in the bins on the street, and eventually in the street itself. I remember walking through New York City late one night and noticing garbage in plastic bags piled everywhere. By early morning all of it was gone, but what if the garbage truck had not come by? When we don't switch off the insulin system, there's no garbage collection in the cells. Toxins build up, damaging the mitochondria, which then do not combust fuel cleanly and produce large amounts of free radicals that further damage the mitochondria.

We fast every night while we sleep. But fasting in preparation for receiving One Spirit Medicine carves out a time between dinner and breakfast so that we turn on the insulin system for no more than eight hours a day.

Generally speaking, however, there's no need to fast from sugars and carbs, including fruit, for more than 18 hours at a time. Brain repair starts to happen that quickly, and brain fog starts to clear. Even during Ramadan, the month-long period of fasting that is one of the most sacred practices of Islam, Muslims fast only from sunrise to sunset each day. As long as you drink plenty of water and refrain from rigorous exercise while you're fasting, you may find that you don't even experience hunger pangs, or if you do, that they're mild enough not to bother you.

Hunger pangs are good; they are an indication that you're switching from the glucose system to the ketone system and your brain is beginning to burn fats. But your limbic brain, the one that runs primarily on sugars, may try to convince you that you'll die if you don't eat a glazed doughnut right away. Don't give in to it. Simply observe this brain going through its machinations, knowing that in fact, your body has enough fuel reserves to get you through the next 40 days without eating—though I don't recommend it!

REDUCING OXIDATIVE STRESS AND FREE-RADICAL ACTIVITY

Mitochondria use oxygen to burn glucose and fats to produce energy to power the body. But like that old car of yours that burned oil and released clouds of black smoke from the exhaust, when metabolism isn't efficient—when it doesn't burn clean—it produces dangerous by-products called free radicals. Free radicals, if you recall, are oxygen atoms that have lost an electron and become unstable. To stabilize themselves, they steal an electron from nearby molecules, which then become free radicals themselves. The total burden placed on the body by free-radical activity is called oxidative stress. A certain amount of free-radical production is normal and even necessary, but when oxidative stress becomes excessive and too many cells are damaged, it accelerates aging and leads to disease.

Environmental toxins worsen the situation by damaging mitochondria. Most dangerous are pesticides, which work by destroying the mitochondria of invasive pests and are designed to stick to the plants and not wash off easily in the rain. Damaged mitochondria produce more free radicals than healthy mitochondria. And then the free radicals damage fats, proteins, and even the DNA in our cell nuclei. Oxidative stress is a vicious cycle.

A diet high in sugar and refined grains increases free-radical production. You can now see why pasta, French fries, cereal, and chocolate cake can be deadly. The more oxidative stress on your body, the more antioxidants you will need to reduce free-radical damage.

You can get antioxidants from foods like berries, but you would need to eat close to 40 pounds of blueberries a day to neutralize the billions of free radicals circulating through your body. Fortunately, the body itself produces antioxidants, and consuming plants like cruciferous vegetables will support the cells' natural ability to manufacture powerful endogenous antioxidants. When you eliminate the foods that poison you and eat healthy, organic foods instead, you reduce the oxidation and inflammation that serve as major stressors on your gut-brain.

INFLAMMATION

Localized inflammation is a natural and healthy immune response. When you fall and scratch your knee, white blood cells deliver plasma and leukocytes to the injury site, trapping foreign matter like bacteria so it can be neutralized and excreted. But chronic inflammation disturbs the body's biochemical equilibrium, and the immune system begins to attack healthy cells and tissues, mistaking them for foreign invaders. This can result in heart disease and autoimmune disorders like rheumatoid arthritis, diabetes, and multiple sclerosis. In the brain, chronic inflammation damages key brain structures, including the hippocampus, leading to conditions like Parkinson's disease, Alzheimer's, and ADHD.

REPAIRING THE HIPPOCAMPUS AND THE NEURAL NETWORKS

Reducing oxidative stress and inflammation repairs the hippocampus. Shaped like a sea horse—*hippos* is Greek for horse—the hippocampus works with the amygdala to modulate emotional responses like anger and fear.

The hippocampus is also the region of the brain associated with learning. Any new skill, from playing a musical instrument to learning to eat for health and longevity, requires the participation of the hippocampus. So when the hippocampus is damaged, learning stops, and curiosity and enthusiasm for life drift away.

The hippocampus is also involved in memory, and damage to it can impair short-term memory while leaving long-term memory intact. That may explain why often people with dementia can recall events from many years in the past yet are unable to remember what happened two weeks or even ten minutes ago.

The hippocampus cannot tell time, so it often confuses something happening today with something similar that happened 20 years ago. That new person we just met may trigger memories of a former lover from years back, and that's where the dialogue ends. And the hippocampus is linked not just to past events but also to old behaviors, worn-out thoughts, and used-up feelings. When it's damaged, we keep experiencing the same painful situations, the same painful moods and feelings, over and over again.

A few years back, a friend invited me to his wedding. It was his fifth wedding ceremony. When I reminded him of this, he told me that this time was different. My friend was trying to repair his hippocampus through yet another marriage—not a very practical way to go about repairing the brain. I explained to him that he had to stop looking for the right partner and start working on *becoming* the right partner. He was not very happy with my advice. Six months after the wedding he called and told me his marriage was over—and he was angry with me that I allowed him to marry such a cruel and thoughtless person. I reminded him of what the scholar and mythologist Joseph Campbell once said: if you don't learn a lesson, you end up marrying it. I told my friend that unless he repaired his hippocampus, he would keep seeking—and finding—the same kind of partner.

When the hippocampus is damaged, it sends messages to the amygdala that the world is dangerous and we might be at risk. Then we respond with survival reflexes that turn everything around us into a threatening situation. When the hippocampus is healed, we begin to see opportunity where we once saw only danger. I have a patient who has made a fortune in the stock market investing in companies that everyone else thought were doomed.

You heal the hippocampus by increasing the level of serotonin and switching on the production of stem cells in the brain. A couple of decades ago we believed that the brain was not able to grow new neurons. Today we know that the brain can produce new stem cells in as little as six weeks, knitting new neural networks and learning fresh ways of looking at life. You can change your life by changing your brain, turning on the production of BDNF—brain-derived neurotrophic factor, a growth hormone—instead of trying to change your life by replacing your spouse, getting a new job, or shipping your kids off to boarding school. However, in order to change your brain, you will need to counteract its tendency to default to its long-established programs for fear, aggression, defensiveness, and other toxic emotions.

Just as updating the operating system on your computer lets you run new, more powerful programs and applications, upgrading your brain sets you up for new, more constructive thinking that can enhance your health and emotional well-being. Nourishing your brain with nutrients and activities that support optimal health will also help you avoid the diseases of aging and modern living. When you become forgetful or have trouble focusing, you may be tempted to laugh off the befuddlement as a "senior moment," while secretly harboring fear of Alzheimer's and dementia, which affect more than half of all octogenarians. The idea that the mind is deteriorating with age is terrifying, but aging does not have to include loss of brain function. The illnesses characteristic of aging in the West, including cardiovascular disease, Alzheimer's, dementia, and Parkinson's, are largely preventable. Prevention starts with repairing the hippocampus and growing new brain cells, along with eating a diet that will fuel your brain with good fats.

BOOSTING BRAIN HEALTH WITH BDNF, GLUTATHIONE, AND SOD

Our Paleolithic ancestors may have known nothing about brain chemistry, but they were savvy about the plants that could switch on the body's ability to repair itself. Now researchers have discovered three key enzymes and proteins that repair the body and brain. Even more amazing is that they turn on the body's ability to produce stem cells and therefore can actually help you grow a new and healthier body!

One enzyme I've already mentioned is **BDNF,** brain-derived neurotrophic factor. It stimulates the development of new brain cells and is vital for repairing and rewiring the brain so that new ways of thinking, perceiving, and responding will emerge spontaneously. When was the last time you fell in love again with your partner or spouse? BDNF updates your brain so you can experience the re-enchantment of your life and your world.

Inadequate BDNF production is associated with Alzheimer's, dementia, and depression. Toxins, stress, lack of exercise, and a sugary diet all lower BDNF levels. If you're not getting enough omega-3s from foods—particularly from fish or fish oils—then supplementing with omega-3 fatty acids is essential to increase BDNF levels and promote production of neural stem cells.

Fasting overnight and then breaking the fast with fats and proteins rather than carbs will increase your BDNF. But to boost it further, you might consider doing a one-day fast every three or four weeks. Exercise is another way to increase BDNF levels, but make sure you choose a form of exercise you enjoy; research shows that exercise you like is better for generating BDNF than something you do only because you know you ought to.

Glutathione is another enzyme that's an antioxidant and an anti-inflammatory. And as a detoxifying agent, it serves as a sort of lint brush, picking up toxins in the body and carrying them to the liver for processing. Glutathione boosts your immunity and helps you build and maintain muscle.

Low glutathione levels increase free-radical damage to the mitochondria, which then produce less energy and are unable to regulate the cells' death clocks. Foods like kale, spinach, avocado, and squash increase the body's ability to manufacture glutathione. However, many people, including me, lack the GSTM1 gene, which is necessary for manufacturing glutathione, and nearly half the world is missing one or more of the genes necessary to produce enough glutathione. Among the critically ill, the percentage is even higher: a majority of people with chronic disease have negligible glutathione levels. Because the body can't utilize glutathione in supplement form—it's easily destroyed in the gut—I recommend the oral form of S-acetyl glutathione, which can make it through the gut and into the bloodstream. I take it twice weekly as a supplement and find it very effective.

SOD, or superoxide dismutase, is the ultimate antioxidant, an enzyme that neutralizes free radicals in a ratio of over a million to one—one molecule of SOD kills one million free radicals. Vitamins C and E are also considered great antioxidants, but they have a kill ratio of only one to one. Since there are zillions of free radicals in the body—far too many for one little vitamin pill to quench—we need the firepower of SOD to effectively reduce damaging oxidative stress.

Low levels of SOD play a role in atherosclerosis—hardening of the arteries associated with aging—and in collagen breakdown in aging skin. Our bodies produce SOD naturally, and it can also be found in foods, but reversing a lifetime of free-radical onslaught from exposure to pesticides and environmental toxins requires a major intervention. You can upgrade your body's ability to manufacture SOD by taking supplements of trans-resveratrol and turmeric. You can also boost SOD by adding pterostilbene-rich foods to your diet—eating more blueberries and grapes, for example—or by taking a pterostilbene supplement. (For more information on supplements, see Chapter 5, Superfoods and Super Supplements.)

While increasing BDNF, glutathione, and SOD can repair your mitochondria and prevent the ravages of the diseases of old age, for the shaman they are important for another reason: they upgrade the brain to be able to experience One Spirit Medicine. The experience of One Spirit allows you to create psychosomatic health and dream their world into being in a powerful and creative way.

CHAPTER 7

FREEING YOURSELF FROM STRESSORS

The major advances in civilization are processes which all but wreck the societies in which they occur.

—ALFRED NORTH WHITEHEAD

Years ago, my mentor Don Jicaram told me that to learn the wisdom of the rain forest, I would have to spend a night alone in the jungle along a tributary of the Amazon River. He dropped me off at a distant beach just as the sun was setting. It was a beautiful spot—a white sandy beach, surrounded by gigantic trees known as *shiwawacos*. Across the river on the other shore, parrots and macaws were feeding on a natural clay lick, getting the minerals that are part of their daily morning and evening meals. The setting sun cast its pale rays on the face of the ocher clay lick, illuminating the blue and red feathers of the birds. And then suddenly, as happens in the jungle in the tropics, it was dark.

I rummaged through my pack and discovered that the old man had taken my flashlight and the matches I always carried for such an occasion. I tried to talk myself into believing that I was in Eden, that there was much beauty all around me, and that I was safe. Yet as night descended, the full awareness of being alone in the dark jungle hit me, and I was terrified. Every snap of a twig or rustling of leaves alarmed me. I was certain I was being stalked by a jaguar that would pounce any second and sink its teeth into me. And then the morning arrived and everything seemed fine again, even after I saw the fresh jaguar tracks in the sand. It wasn't until I had spent much more time in the rain forest that I understood that I could be safe there even with minimal provisions. I learned not to be prey for jaguars.

We become prey for jaguars and others who would devour us when they smell our fear. A jaguar can track your scent from miles away, just as a mugger in the inner city can pick you out as his target with an uncanny sense of knowing which people are easy marks. Fear launches a chemical cascade that literally changes your scent to that of a hunted animal. Then your emotional state casts the world as predatory, and you focus on self-protection: *Am I safe? Do I have enough love, or money, or whatever else I need to feel secure?* Fear keeps you in a chronic hyperalert state that can turn you into a victim—and someone's dinner.

Our emotions can make us sick. Shamans understand that most of the problems we face are caused by our unhealed emotions. Emotions are ancient survival programs encoded in the limbic brain, and when toxic emotions dominate your thinking and nervous system, you put yourself in danger. To stop being the victim of your circumstances and become a hero embarking on an epic journey of discovery, you will need to heal your emotions. You won't have to go out of your way to find opportunities to heal.

Life presents plenty of challenges and stressors that will allow you to rewire the neural pathways in your brain, transforming toxic emotions like fear and anger into positive feelings like compassion and love.

Shamans distinguish between toxic emotions, which can fester and poison us, and feelings, which are of the moment and transitory. You might have an occasional feeling of anger toward your children or spouse, a spontaneous flash that sends a surge of chemicals through your body and brain, but the feeling passes soon and equanimity returns. Toxic emotions, on the other hand, can linger in the body and limbic brain for hours or days or years. The brain scientist Jill Bolte Taylor describes the difference between feeling and emotion in *My Stroke of Insight: A Brain Scientist's Personal Journey*: "Within 90 seconds from the initial trigger, the chemical component of my anger has completely dissipated from my blood and my automatic response is over. If, however, I remain angry after those 90 seconds have passed, then it is because I have *chosen* to let that circuit continue to run. Moment by moment, I make the choice to either hook into my neurocircuitry or move back into the present moment . . ."[1]

Fear is one of the deadliest emotions. It blinds us to opportunities around us. Terror sees no way out. Fear triggers the fight-or-flight system, known as the HPA axis, which consists of the hypothalamus and the pituitary gland, pea-size structures in the brain, and the adrenal glands, which sit atop the kidneys. When you sense danger, perceived or real, the brain launches a distress response in the HPA axis, reducing the blood flow to your prefrontal cortex, the part of the brain that can see possibilities.

There are real dangers in the world. But you have a choice about how you respond to them. To stop being prey, you need to let go of beliefs that reinforce your view of the world as predatory. Once you understand that it is your beliefs that cause stress and not people or situations "out there," you will be able to live in harmony with the world around you instead of feeling as if you're trapped forever in a combat zone.

The emotional stress we experience in everyday life is often the result of our limiting beliefs and an overactive fight-or-flight response.

LIMITING BELIEFS

Our assumptions about the world can cause emotional stress in ways we aren't aware of. Limiting beliefs have nothing to do with IQ or education and everything to do with early life experiences that shape our worldview, which the brain's ever-efficient yet unconscious neural networks interpret as reality. It sometimes seems as if the more knowledgeable experts are, the more likely they are to be blinded by their beliefs. Before the U.S. invaded Iraq, countless experts testified that Saddam Hussein was stockpiling weapons of mass destruction; later, of course, none were found. The "facts" presented to the American people were bogus. The experts who testified before Congress were not lying; they were simply convinced they had a lock on the truth.

In forming an opinion, we give weight to facts that fit with our beliefs and readily dismiss those that don't. Western society favors science and reason over intuition, seldom blending the two different ways of knowing to gain a broader perspective. When I talk to people who have a medical background, they always want to know the scientific research that supports my statements about health, even when they instinctively know what I'm saying is true. That's one reason I've included so much science in a book about ancient shamanic medicine: we want to see research papers published in professional journals that validate age-old advice.

The more we rely exclusively on one way of knowing, however, the more likely we are to operate from biases we aren't even aware of. Our insistence on valuing science over intuition ignores findings that when we combine the two, we often make better decisions. A ten-year study of ESP in business executives by researchers Douglas Dean and John Mihalasky found that CEOs who trusted intuition and took risks based on their hunches made significantly more money than CEOs who made decisions based solely on logic and "facts."[2] And intuition isn't necessarily as irrational as hard-core rationalists assume. Nobel prizewinners Herbert Simon and Daniel Kahneman are among those whose research has found that when experts make decisions based on intuition, they're actually drawing on a storehouse of experience and knowledge.[3] By contrast, a decision made on a hunch, like *I don't know why I chose him; I just liked his look,* is more likely a purely emotional response and has as much chance of being wrong as being right. The shamans I've met are certainly expert healers, and what they're drawing on is the stored wisdom of generations of the elders, and shared experience in co-creating with Spirit.

A common bias that can have grave consequences is the belief that we aren't equipped to address our own health needs but must rely on doctors, drugs, and therapies to heal us. This leads to a feeling of powerlessness that can prevent us from taking lifesaving action on our own behalf. One Spirit Medicine helps us recognize that we don't need to depend on medical experts or drugs alone. We can draw on the power of the mind and Spirit to support our innate self-healing ability. We can choose to release negative emotions that feed depression, anger, and worry, and cultivate positive emotions that help the body repair.

As long as we're caught in the grip of our limiting beliefs stored in the limbic brain, we will constantly look to others to tell us what to do—not just medical experts to determine our health care but also political commentators to tell us how to vote and the media to show us who our enemies are.

Limiting beliefs tend to keep us trapped in one of three roles: victim, persecutor, or rescuer. These sit at the three corners of what I call the triangle of disempowerment. We create dramas featuring these stock roles, and then as the story unfolds, we act as if lost in a maze, never breaking out of the disempowering tale. Small wonder every situation seems familiar: we keep projecting the same parts onto the players and reenacting the old dramas.

Whether victim or persecutor or rescuer, we are continually reacting to the actions of others. We see this wherever people are driven by limiting beliefs. To the Westernized Indians I visited in South America, the persecutors were the conquistadors, the Indians were the victims, and the rescuer was the Catholic Church.

New patients who come to see me for shamanic energy medicine often want me to be the rescuer who heals them from whatever disease is keeping them a victim. My first task is to refuse that job and instead help the patients break out of their limiting beliefs and find their own inner power to heal. Otherwise they will expect me to perform magic while they remain passive observers.

All these roles—victim, persecutor, rescuer—keep us feeling scared, defensive, envious, and competitive. When we encounter someone who is doing something clever or original, instead of admiring that person, we feel jealous, or we belittle their efforts. Like the writer Gore Vidal is credited with saying, "Every time a friend of mine succeeds, a little part of me dies." The opportunity we face in healing our emotions is to move beyond our limiting beliefs and understand our lives in a larger context, unfettered by biases that distort our perceptions. Heroic narratives about people who have been tested and then overcome their wounds to heal themselves and their communities are far more empowering than the three-character dramas we habitually create.

OVERSTIMULATION AND FIGHT-OR-FLIGHT

Two stressors we face today—overstimulation and an overactive fight-or-flight system—often go hand in hand. We're bombarded with more information and sensory stimulation than we can possibly handle, which sets off our HPA axis, our fight-or-flight response.

From television and the Internet alone, we're exposed to more stimuli in a week than our Paleolithic ancestors were exposed to in a lifetime. And we're continually running to keep up with new information, to the point that we're chronically exhausted. I can't count how many times I have heard someone say, "If it weren't for caffeine, I wouldn't get anything done!" Nature designed the brain to deal with only one lion roaring at us at a time, not the entire jungle turning against us. Now, however, our brain is too overtaxed to spend time sorting through all the data, much less looking at it with fresh eyes and deciding what is or is not a crisis, and what, if anything, needs to be done about it.

The media bring us news about wars and devastation happening in distant lands, but our fight-or-flight response operates only with local coordinates, and doesn't understand *far away.* When we read about some catastrophic event, the thinking part of our brain grasps that it's happening at another time and place. But the brain perceives images nonverbally and much faster. So when the hippocampus, which regulates the fight-or-flight response, is presented with streaming video of an atrocity, it registers it as happening now and nearby, and goes on high alert. The more damaged the hippocampus is by stress and toxins, the closer and more threatening the danger seems to be.

I'm convinced that hippocampus damage on a national scale can be measured by the number of guns owned by a country's citizens. According to *The Washington Post,* the U.S. has the highest per capita gun ownership in the world—nearly 90 guns for every 100 people—and the highest rate of gun-related murders in the developed world.[4] The hippocampus senses danger lurking behind every tree.

Another reason why our fight, flight, or freeze response is perennially on—"freeze" is the response of an overloaded HPA axis—is the speed with which we have to react to incoming information. Our feelings are conveyed by hormones traveling through the body in a slow, analog chemical system. You can bask in the feeling of love toward a child or a pet, or seethe in anger for days. Our thoughts, on the other hand, course through our nervous system at the speed of light, in digital electrical signals demanding an immediate response. Therefore, in our information-overloaded, super-caffeinated society, there is an ever-widening gap between our thoughts and our feelings, our heads and our guts, and overstimulation is the result. We sleep but do not rest. We are chronically exhausted and overworked. And this stress keeps the

HPA axis running nonstop, stuck in the *on* position, poisoning the brain with stress hormones that leave us paralyzed in fear or felled by chronic exhaustion.

You've probably heard the expression, "Neurons that fire together wire together." For many people today, the neural pathways in the brain for fight-or-flight have widened into superhighways. According to the National Institute of Mental Health, in any given year some 25 percent of Americans qualify for a mental health diagnosis, and of those, 18 percent have anxiety and 7 percent depression.[5] Sadly, among teenagers, anxiety and depression are five to eight times as prevalent today as they were 50 years ago.[6]

The hippocampus is, in effect, the thermostat of the HPA axis. It sets the threshold for what we consider danger, what we see as opportunity, and what we dismiss as mundane. The higher it sets the thermostat, the less likely we are to feel spooked and the less dangerous our world seems. But when the thermostat is set low, it takes very little heat to trigger the fight-or-flight mechanism. On constant alert, we see danger everywhere.

And the HPA axis doesn't just control our responses to danger; it's also involved in regulating digestion, mood, sexuality, energy storage, and the immune system—which makes compromising it all the more life threatening. When our fight-or-flight response is engaged, the HPA axis produces adrenaline and cortisol, powerful steroid hormones. We can actually become addicted to fear and overstimulation—or more precisely, to the chemicals they induce. It's easy to mistake a rush of adrenaline for vitality. The difference is that vitality is rejuvenating, whereas stress chemicals flooding the system lead to burnout, and damage our tissues and organs, including the brain.

The hippocampus is rich in cortisol receptors, and when the adrenal gland floods the system with cortisol in response to stress, it can damage the hippocampus. But by nourishing the brain with omega-3 fatty acids, you can repair the hippocampus and reset the fight-or-flight response. In as little as six weeks of taking omega-3s, you can begin to see beauty where you saw only ugliness and sense opportunity where you perceived only danger. The hippocampus repairs quickly, and when you stop feeding your brain adrenaline and caffeine, you start to free yourself from the negative effects of stress.

When the fight-or-flight system is quiet, the alchemical laboratory in the pineal gland begins to assemble endogenous psychedelics that flood the brain, creating states of joy, bliss, and communion. The brain cannot manufacture the molecules for fear and stress and produce the psychedelics for bliss at the same time. It's either one or the other.

It's essential to stop taking in so much stimulation and consciously build in downtime—minutes, hours, even days free of mental and emotional drama. Meditating, immersing yourself fully in a pleasurable activity, or simply spending time in nature can be great stress relievers. Whenever you feel overwhelmed, you can stop and take a few deep breaths.

I have a patient who was a terrible lover. At least that's what his wife claimed. She said that for him sex was like feeding a deep hunger that he tried to satisfy as quickly as possible. He focused only on the climax, missing the shared pleasures of foreplay. His drive to be the first to the finish line, which served him so well in his work as an investment banker, made him a loser in bed. He was unable to slow down and appreciate the intimacy. The couple came to see me after six months of unsuccessful marital therapy, and the first thing I did was put them both on a clinical dose of omega-3s, three to five grams a day. With that and some coaching from his wife, the man was able to discover the prize of sensual exploration and discovery. But the omega-3s were only part of his treatment. We also used a shamanic technique to reset his fight-or-flight response. Once we reset his HPA axis, he no longer froze in bed, and was able to explore intimacy with his partner.

When we let go of the addiction to the adrenaline and dopamine that keep us fired up and ready for battle, we can live more wisely. The hasty decisions and fear-fueled, impulsive actions we later regret happen less frequently when the HPA axis mechanism is not running the show. It's only when the brain is stuck in fight-or-flight mode that it defaults to the old toxic stories that lead us to act in clichéd, unproductive, even destructive ways, caught in the triangle of disempowerment.

Freed from fight-or-flight mode, we can begin to dream again—not just at night but also during the day. Hunter-gatherers invest only about three hours a day in procuring food, and devote the rest of their time to leisure, art, and dreaming. The Hadza of Tanzania, like the !Kung of Botswana, work only about 14 hours a week. But once our forbears started farming, the amount of time devoted to ensuring they had enough food on their plates increased so much there was almost no time for sitting around the fire and exchanging stories. Industrialization was no help; time became even scarcer as workers slaved long hours in factories. It was only the people near the top or the bottom of the hierarchies of power—the super rich or the indigent monks—who were able to devote themselves to contemplation. Even now, it's difficult to meditate and daydream creatively when your days are eaten up by e-mails and laundry.

But the importance of daydreaming cannot be overestimated. James H. Simons, a math genius of breathtaking accomplishment who started a hedge fund that made him a billionaire and a major donor to scientific causes, attributes his success to "pondering." "I wasn't the fastest guy in the world," he told *The New York Times*. "But I like to ponder. And pondering things, just sort of thinking about [them] turns out to be a pretty good approach."[7]

Gazing at the stars and imagining what might be has largely been replaced by working through an endless To Do list. Dreaming and just *being* have been pushed aside in the name of *doing*. We stand outdoors glued to our smartphones, scrolling through text-message alerts and checking the temperature on our weather apps, instead of feeling the sun and the wind on our skin.

Technology gives us access to plenty of information. As long as we're close to a wireless hot spot, any point of contention can be settled instantly by pulling out a digital device and doing a search. What we lack is the capacity to tame all that information and experience true wisdom. Information compels us to take action—to buy, sell, perform. Wisdom compels us to dream.

In the West we're clever at managing information by specializing. A physician may know about the gastrointestinal tract in exhaustive detail but be clueless when it comes to human emotions. Psychologists treating patients for depression or anxiety almost never think to ask about GI problems, even though many mood disorders originate in the gut. We practice medicine by geography, with doctors specializing in hearts or brains or bones or colons but seldom putting it all together into a holistic view of the patient's wellness.

OVERCOMING FEAR OF DEATH

Limiting beliefs, overstimulation, an overactive fight-or-flight response—the mental and emotional stressors we experience all lead to our most primal fear of all: fear of death. In aboriginal societies there are rites of passage and initiations carefully designed to confront a person directly with the terror of facing death. The idea is that in experiencing death ritually, you overcome fear of that ultimate, inevitable loss. The shamans call it "living through your death," and it awakens deep wisdom about non-ordinary reality, the continuity of life in the unseen world. After that you are no longer plagued by a chronic sense of anxiety about everyday matters and can hold a larger vision of your purpose in life.

As your brain is upgraded, you will discover that you can let go of your fixation on what you think is absolutely vital to your safety and happiness, essential for your survival. As you release your old, fear-fueled approach to life, you will find you have more faith in your ability to handle uncertainty. You will gain a sense of living in a world that is safe and welcoming, and a universe that supports your intentions.

SEPARATION VERSUS UNITY

The limbic brain perceives separation rather than unity. It breaks reality into bite-size pieces in order to understand it, but in doing so, it misses the whole. By contrast, the higher brain senses that the visible world of matter and physical phenomena and the invisible world of Spirit and energy are not separate. It is only our practical, everyday perception that draws a distinction between the two. In the visible world, I perceive that my body is separate from the body of the person sitting in the chair next to me. But in the invisible world, everything is interwoven, indivisible.

The invisible world is unified, nonlocal, and beyond space-time. Though omnipresent, it is invisible to ordinary perception: we know it only through its manifestations. We can directly apprehend the invisible realm only when our perception shifts, and the space-time barrier between the two worlds momentarily drops away.

Until you glimpse non-ordinary, invisible reality, your brain will remain biased toward separation and fearing "what's out there." After you experience One Spirit Medicine, the sense of separation dissolves, as you perceive yourself to be an inextricable part of the larger whole.

After taking One Spirit Medicine, you can dream health and wellness into being, envision freedom from scarcity and fear, and picture harmonious interactions with other people, other creatures, and the planet. You discover that death is not something to be feared and avoided at any cost, but merely a doorway to another realm.

In the ordinary, visible world, our possibilities are limited by the information our senses can grasp. Our minds are trained to match up what we encounter today with what we've experienced in the past. But in the non-ordinary world, you can access the primordial soup of all creation, unlimited in its potential for giving birth to the new. Seeming impossibilities become possible.

It was the wisdom of the invisible world that fueled the courage of ancient people to sail toward the horizon and settle Australia 50,000 years ago, and to set out on foot toward the unknown and cross the Bering Strait into North America. When you draw on the wisdom of the non-ordinary realm, you can conceive of a world of endless possibility and help shape a future that hasn't gotten around to revealing itself.

The big ideas, the ones that are in synch with who we can be as opposed to who we think we ought to be, come from the non-ordinary realm. They may sound batty to people who are identified with the ordinary world and its limitations, but the energy of these ideas is too powerful, too compelling to ignore.

If you have the courage, One Spirit Medicine can pull you into an entirely different life, one with new health, new wisdom, new activities, new relationships, new opportunities. You'll begin to feel more at home in your own skin. Changes you make will stick, and nothing will deter you from following your dreams.

PART IV

FROM
STILLNESS
COMES
REBIRTH

CHAPTER 8

EMBRACING A NEW MYTHOLOGY

Religions, philosophies, arts, the social forms
of primitive and historic man, prime discoveries
in science and technology, the very dreams that
blister sleep, boil up from the basic, magic ring of myth.

—JOSEPH CAMPBELL

First you eliminated the poisons in your body and upgraded your brain with superfoods and neuro-nutrients. Then you began to free yourself from toxic emotions and limiting beliefs, resetting fight-or-flight and turning on the production of the spirit molecules in your brain. The next step toward receiving One Spirit Medicine is to improve the quality of your gene expression, turning on the genes for health and turning off the genes for disease. For this you will need to hack into the password-protected codes of the luminous energy field (LEF) that surrounds the physical body. You can get to the LEF when you let go of the familial and cultural stories and conflicts that confine you to a constricted experience of life. You can then adopt a new, more encompassing mythology that supports your ability to dream a new body and a new world into being.

Why mythology? Because the right side of the neocortex, the higher brain, operates on stories and myths, not facts. The success of TV series like *Game of Thrones,* films like *The Lord of the Rings* and *Star Wars,* and the Harry Potter books attest to our fascination with fantasy and myth. At the same time we tend to underestimate the power of myths, dismissing them as charming fables or entertaining tales. But as the scholar Joseph Campbell made clear, myths aren't just plotlines for comic books and summer block-buster movies. They affect us to a far greater degree and at a far deeper level than we realize. From a very young age, we fall under the spell of powerful myths that influence the way we perceive the world and, consequently, the choices we make every day.

Mythologies represent the beliefs and values of particular groups or cultures. To a large extent, the guiding myths of the West differ from those in other parts of the world. Certain myths, however, seem to be universal, written on the collective human psyche and conveying archetypal energies that crosscut time and geography. The most enduring myths involve ordinary people embarking on heroic quests, often against their will, and overcoming apparently insurmountable obstacles to perform extraordinary deeds.

The myths of the ancient Greeks centered on the all-too-human antics of the gods on Mount Olympus and the exploits of heroes like Odysseus, Hercules, and Achilles. Our modern myths are no less compelling than those of the ancient Greeks and Romans. A classic American myth is the rags-to-riches tale of the self-made man who rises to fame and fortune through determination and hard work. Hand in hand with that is the myth of the plucky orphan, who overcomes a challenging and loveless childhood thanks to her courage, dignity, and winsome charm. Like all good myths, these stories end in triumph, with virtue rewarded. Narratives like these fueled the entrepreneurial aspirations of Americans right through the end of the 20th century, when a new breed of stock trader and Internet wunderkind amassed billions overnight.

The mythic tales of the 21st century point to a different set of values. Now our myths are flights of fantasy, set in faraway star systems or magical lands inhabited by dragons, wizards, and otherworldly beings. Or they reflect the shadow side of fantasy—dark, apocalyptic visions of devastation. Either way, we're no longer in thrall to Horatio Alger and Little Orphan Annie. But the underlying theme remains the same: an ordinary person is called to face extraordinary challenges and is transformed in the process.

The values and beliefs contained in myths are so strong that once you find your personal guiding myth, you feel compelled to change your life to conform to it. Change the myth and your values and beliefs change—and the facts of your life change accordingly.

But you can only change your personal myth after you've upgraded your brain, because a broken brain automatically runs the old software, leaving you at the mercy of the four ancient programs of the limbic brain: fighting, fleeing, feeding, and fornicating. When we're caught up in aggression, fear, or greed—or its opposite, scarcity—we're unable to adopt new values and beliefs, even in the face of a serious crisis. Unconscious programming overrides our best intentions.

The Judeo-Christian traditions of the West have left us with powerful myths that operate in the psyche like computer programs running continually in the background. We're not even aware of them, but they drive our basic sense of self-worth and our vision of the world, coloring the way we live from day to day.

One of the first Bible stories we learn as children is that of Adam and Eve in the Book of Genesis. The myth of Adam and Eve freights us with original sin, telling us that because we disobeyed God, we're banished forever from the Garden of Eden and can no longer commune directly with God—or with the rivers and rocks and trees and animals. But indigenous peoples, whether sub-Saharan Africans or Australian aboriginals or Native Americans, hold no such belief about expulsion from paradise. In their mythologies not only were they *not* kicked out of the Garden but they were given the Garden and entrusted with maintaining it, as the caretakers of earth. We may say we want to live more sustainably, in harmony with the natural world, but our old, ingrained belief system continually hijacks our goal. We rationalize that as individuals we can't make a difference, or that the world economy would collapse if we endorsed the Kyoto Protocol limiting emissions of greenhouse gasses. So we end up pursuing short-term economic stability and do nothing about reversing climate change.

Our Judeo-Christian tradition has also given us a number of other myths we've internalized, not least the idea that eternal life is for only the chosen few—and that the priests hold our passports to heaven. Such a view would be inconceivable to the indigenous peoples I've lived with. To them, heaven is on earth, no one is excluded, and existence is eternal; death is simply a passage from one state to another, from our "particle" nature to our "wave" nature. Eastern philosophies like Buddhism hold a similar view: consciousness is eternal, and paradise is an awakened state here on earth, accessible to all.

To the shamans, eternity is available to anyone who upgrades their brain and grows a new, improved body through One Spirit Medicine. Ultimate healing is not of the physical body only but of the luminous energy field—the light body that takes us beyond this life to the end of time. This is the body of light that we will keep with us for a very long time after this life ends, and that we neglect entirely in the West.

Another persistent myth we labor under is a belief in evil as an independent principle in the universe. But far more compelling to me is the view that we live in a benevolent universe that will go out of its way to conspire on our behalf, if we are in right relationship with it.

These old stories linger in what the psychiatrist Carl Jung called the collective unconscious, the repository of ideas and memories shared by the species. The collective mythology runs so deep that we seldom stop to think, *This story has gotten old.* It generally takes global crises, game-changing technologies, and radical discoveries to replace the old myths with new ones. Just as the invention of the printing press altered the collective mythology in the centuries that followed, the world wide web is a transforming narrative of our age. In adopting a new mythology we can alter the forces affecting our lives, preparing us individually to receive One Spirit Medicine and collectively to create a more sustainable future for the planet.

ARCHETYPAL ENERGIES

At this point in our history, it's pretty clear that the human species needs to be more collaborative, creative, and cooperative—qualities that are aspects of the archetypal mother figure. To bring balance back into our relationship with Mother Earth and with one another, we need to replace the masculine mythology of domination, conquest, and hierarchical power. And on a personal level, we need to overcome the self-focused, power-hungry, battle-fixated limbic mind-set.

It's not enough to simply promise ourselves we'll change. We have to actively engage archetypal energies that will reorient our beliefs and values and actions. The archetypes we need to draw on are, in fact, very ancient. They have guided and influenced human experience throughout time. Carl Jung described archetypes as "forms in the psyche which seem to be present always and everywhere."[1] Archetypes are embedded in mythology handed down through oral tradition, wisdom teachings, and sacred books, and woven into religious and secular rituals. In fact, mythology and folklore based on tales of human interaction with archetypal forces—the gods of old—have existed in every culture on earth since humans first developed language.

The stories that have power for us incorporate universal themes that touch us deeply. Whether we're reading the myth of Odysseus, or watching a love story on the big screen, or listening to a song about a man who wins his beloved through perseverance, we respond to a narrative that speaks to our longing and dreams. We close the book, walk out of the theater, or turn off the music feeling uplifted—inspired to enjoy every moment of our all-too-brief life.

When we constantly expose ourselves to the old, disempowering myths that have wormed their way into books, movies, and newscasts, we end up reliving them by default. We get caught up in desperately competing with a younger rival; we fall prey to a clever trickster; we repeat habits that make us physically sick, psychologically unwell, and spiritually bereft. Our perception narrows to the tried-and-true, and we lose the ability to creatively interact with life. Stuck in crisis, we fail to recognize an opportunity to view a rival as a partner, or a trickster as a potential playmate.

Not too long ago, on an expedition I led to the Andes Mountains, one of the participants, Mark, felt very threatened by the indigenous mythology we were exploring. He is a successful stockbroker who believes that there are only so many slices to the pie and you have to grab yours before someone else does. The shamans we were working with pointed out that Mark was accumulating slices of the wrong pie. He was going after the pie that would bring him more wealth, but the Great Pie, they said, is in the sky: it's the pie of wisdom and generosity, and there are plenty of slices to go around. "Even the squirrels know when they have stored enough nuts for the winter," the shamans told him.

Their message struck Mark like a slap in the face, and he came to me angry and frustrated, claiming that the Indians only wanted his money, that they were trying to sell him stones and feathers and cloths for their own personal benefit and gain. He wanted to leave the expedition right away. Fortunately, we were high in the mountains, and there was no way to get down to the valley until the following day. I suggested that what was really upsetting Mark was the realization that no amount of wealth, fame, or notoriety could ever fill his heart and soul. Reluctantly, he agreed that might be true. He acknowledged that his definition of success was limited and that he had to widen his perspective if he hoped to find any peace of mind.

Updating your personal mythology means abandoning the seductive yet limiting beliefs that affect us collectively and create for each of us a living hell. Mark's belief was that he could help the world only after he became very rich; then he would donate money to charities he liked. It was a shock to realize that he had to start with changing himself and his personal myth of scarcity. Changing your personal myths requires interacting with familiar stories in new ways so that you can use those energies more wisely and efficiently. You could revise how you engage with your inner warrior, for example, by giving up violence toward yourself and others, and reserving your adversarial energy for only the most essential battles and the athletic field.

We can become warriors who fight our own demons instead of looking for people to demonize and dominate. We can wage holy war on the infidel within—or even chuck the warrior energy altogether and see what our inner infidel has to teach us. In similar fashion, we could work with the pouting inner child who always wants things our way, or the jealous Aphrodite who demands that all attention and adoration be focused on us.

EXERCISE
FINDING AN EMPOWERING MYTHOLOGY

Personal myths are deep and unconscious programs that reveal themselves through dreams and fairy tales. Each of us is the hero or heroine of our own personal mythology, but if your guiding myths are keeping you tied to a limited and disempowering worldview, then finding a new, more empowering personal mythology is essential for your health and well-being.

- The first step to finding a new narrative is to identify the old myths and stories that no longer serve you. Write a short fairy tale—no more than one page—about a man or woman locked up in a castle dungeon. How did the prisoner come to be there? What are the beliefs and fears keeping him or her there?

- Sit quietly and allow a new vision for yourself and your life to emerge. Write a new story in which you are free, leaving the castle for the unknown, meeting challenges and opportunities, crafting a new destiny. Identify the strengths and beliefs on which your new narrative is based.

MOVING TOWARD A NEW MYTHOLOGY

In the next four chapters, we'll look at four myths that illustrate the power that comes with embracing a new personal mythology. The stories of Parsifal, Psyche, Arjuna, and Siddhartha map the steps of the journey to break free of limiting beliefs and change our destinies. Each of these individuals embarked on a heroic journey of transformation in which they became godlike and divine.

Our vehicle for working with these myths and claiming their power is the medicine wheel, a teaching tool from indigenous peoples of the Americas that is integral to all earth-based spiritual traditions. These traditions honor the feminine principle, the Mother archetype, and a relationship with Spirit.

Stonehenge in England and Machu Picchu in Peru—ancient sites sacred to the indigenous peoples of Britain and the Andes, respectively —are perhaps the most famous examples of spirituality grounded in the land and the cycles of nature. Dominant features of both sites are massive stones oriented to the yearly movement of the sun as it traverses the sky from spring equinox to summer solstice to autumn equinox to winter solstice, then begins its journey again.

The medicine wheel provides a map for tackling the challenges of transformation. As we work our way around the wheel in the four directions—from South to West to North to East—we learn to live more courageously and creatively, in preparation for receiving the healing of One Spirit Medicine.

Though the practices associated with the medicine wheel vary among the different indigenous groups of North and South America, the way I was taught by my teachers in the Amazon, we begin in the South, with the journey of the healer and healing our past wounds. We then move to the West and the journey of the Divine Feminine, facing the fear of death. From there we move to the North, the journey of the sage, where we learn to be still, like the surface of the lake that reflects everything and disturbs nothing. Finally, we reach the East and the journey of the visionary, where we practice dreaming the world into being and participating in creation.

This is the classic hero's journey, calling us to leave our ordinary life as we know it and step fearlessly into the unknown.

The journey to One Spirit Medicine is a solo journey, in that no one can do the work of transformation for you. But that does not mean you walk the medicine wheel alone. You embark on this path as part of a courageous community of men and women of wisdom who have come before you. Help from the universe is always available, but we have to humble ourselves to benefit from its assistance. Without humility, we will almost certainly slip back into our old ways, into the same disempowering, me-centered stories. The ego wants to take a quick turn around the medicine wheel and be completely healed, but that is not the way transformation works. With patience and dedication, we have to master the lessons of each direction before we can receive One Spirit Medicine.

Once you've completed the work of the medicine wheel, you are ready for the vision quest, the final action step in the journey to receive One Spirit Medicine.

CHAPTER 9

THE JOURNEY OF THE HEALER:

SHEDDING THE PAST AND HEALING OUR MOTHER WOUNDS

There comes a time in every man's life when he must encounter his past. For those who are dreamed, who have no more than a passing acquaintance with power, this moment is usually played out from their deathbeds as they try to bargain with fate for a few more moments of lifetime.

But for the dreamer, the person of power, this moment takes place alone, before a fire, when he calls upon the specters of his personal past to stand before him like witnesses before the court. This is the work of the healer, where the medicine wheel begins.

In the Southern Hemisphere, the home of the earth-based traditions of the Andes, the Southern Cross constellation occupies a prominent place in the psyche as well as in the sky, much as the Big Dipper and North Star guide residents of the Northern Hemisphere. The four stars in the Southern Cross orient the stargazer and symbolically reflect the progression through the four stages of the medicine wheel that culminate in One Spirit Medicine. The journey of the healer starts in the South on the medicine wheel.

The South is considered the domain of the serpent: in indigenous cosmology, the Milky Way is the Sky Serpent. In all cultures the serpent archetype represents sexuality and the life force. Eastern traditions associate the serpent with *kundalini,* a vital force often depicted as a snake coiled at the base of the spine. The serpent represents the instincts and literal thinking; everything is just as we see it, without nuance or ambiguity, summed up in the expression *It is what it is.* In this mode, feeling and emotion are not involved. Like the cold-blooded serpent, we act unsentimentally.

In some situations, seeing through the eyes of the serpent is exactly what's needed. When you're in danger and fear might cause you to panic and make bad choices, acting instinctually can ensure your survival. If you're standing on an open mountaintop with lightning striking around you, it is not a time for reflection but for your serpent instinct to kick in and tell you to find safe ground.

The serpent reminds us of our connection to the earth, the source of our sustenance and support. The physical realm of flesh, soil, and rocks awakens our senses as, like the snake, we outgrow our old skins and leave them behind. The work of the healer is to shed the roles and identities that no longer serve you and trust that you can survive without them. Staying in touch with what your body is sensing, you can act instinctively without deliberating about what to do. A pregnant woman in labor doesn't ruminate on whether or not to give birth; she trusts in her body's innate wisdom and surrenders to the contractions.

Serpent impels us to move forward when we need to shed old identities and make a radical change. If we get stuck in serpent awareness, however, we live mindlessly, concerned with our own well-being and survival without regard for the feelings or needs of others. We cling to what we know—the identities and roles that served us in the past. Very often, these are identities shaped more by our social conditioning and the influence of our parents than by any conscious choice on our part. Because the primitive reptilian brain finds comfort in familiarity, under its influence we avoid change, even when the old roles no longer suit. A man marries yet hesitates to leave his bachelor lifestyle behind. A woman marries yet has difficulty moving away from her family to establish a home of her own. Someone recovers from a life-threatening illness yet remains a patient, vulnerable and afraid.

When our eyes are on yesterday, we aren't able to recognize possibilities right in front of us. And just as the eyesight of a snake becomes less acute when it's about to shed its skin, our perception tends to narrow as we resist needed change. Seeing danger, not opportunity, we miss the chance to experiment with new ways of being that might make us happier or lead to greater self-discovery.

Robin, a woman in her late 30s who was the mother of two teenage boys, came to me for shamanic healing at a crisis point in her life. She was distraught because her teenage sons now seemed to need her only to do their laundry and clean their rooms. Yet she had no identity other than "Mom," and as upset as she was that her role had devolved into being her children's maid, she was even more terrified of what her life would be like if she tried something else—perhaps a job in advertising, her previous career. Robin knew how to design magazine ads for women's clothing, but the field had gone on without her, and she knew nothing about Internet marketing, search engine optimization, or virtual storefronts.

When she came to my office, Robin complained that life at home was making her angry and sick: she had gained 30 pounds and whenever she tried to discipline her sons, her heart started racing and she felt a headache coming on. Every morning she woke up in a daze, unable to think clearly without several cups of coffee. She knew she had to change. I asked her to begin by eating the omega-3 rich brain foods that repair the hippocampus, explaining that this would help her break free of the old thinking that kept her locked in her role as mother and maid long past the point of it being helpful to her children or to her. I also asked her to stay away from gluten and dairy for a month, to see if she was reacting to either one, and to avoid sugar and refined carbs.

In our next session three weeks later, I performed an Illumination to clear old imprints from the luminous energy field. Afterward, I lit a large candle that I keep on my desk. I asked Robin to write her most uncomfortable roles on small pieces of paper, then to take each piece, roll it up, blow a prayer into it, and then hold the stick in the flame as it burned. Just as her fingertips were beginning to feel the heat from the flame she was to drop the burning stick into a metal bowl I had filled with sand. This ritual, I explained, was a way of consciously releasing the worn-out roles that were informing her old identity by symbolically reducing them to ashes.

The first role she wanted to release was *maid*. "I am so done with that one!" she practically shouted. Then she burned the roles of *short-order cook, laundrywoman, wife,* and finally *advertising manager.* In shedding that role from her earlier career, she opened herself up to a new role that incorporated both the changes in her industry and the changes in herself. She hoped to use her skills in a new way—perhaps in advertising, perhaps in another field.

Shamans have long known what neuroscientists are now confirming—the power of ritual to change the brain. Small rituals like the one Robin used help you lift your awareness out of your literal, limbic brain into your higher-order neural networks. As Robin committed her old roles to the fire, she let out a big sigh of relief. However, she decided to keep one role—*mother.* "I will be their mom all my life, but no longer the maid," she explained. Had Robin burned her old roles without first repairing her hippocampus, this exercise would have been little more than a quaint gesture based on good intentions. Good intentions are easily forgotten, and willpower can dwindle away, making it extremely difficult to truly shift your mind-set or behavior.

After our session, Robin went home and informed all the men in her family, including her husband, that she was going back to school to learn about Internet marketing. If they wanted to eat, they would have to cook for themselves. If they wanted clean laundry, they would have to learn how to operate the washer and dryer. And Robin stuck with her decision. For two weeks, her house was a disaster area, with dirty dishes and dirty clothes everywhere. But then hunger and hygiene made the men in her household rise to the occasion.

In the journey of the healer, you have to trust that just as the serpent is protected by nature as it sheds its skin, your soft, vulnerable underbelly will be safe without the roles and identities you discard. As the oldest student in her class at the local community college, Robin found her new direction frightening. And she had to restrain herself from rescuing her husband and boys from their mess. But repairing her hippocampus, the brain center associated with new learning, allowed her not only to release her old roles but also to acquire new skills that would help her thrive as a marketing executive rather than simply survive as a housekeeper.

Robin and I also worked to change her image of the mother archetype from that of a giant breast nursing everyone in perpetuity to a mother jaguar cuffing her grown cubs with a firm paw to show them when it's time to leave the den.

PARSIFAL AND HEALING THE MASCULINE

The legend of Parsifal, a knight of King Arthur's Round Table, illustrates the archetypal quest for wholeness and healing, the struggle to let go of the identities of the past in order to evolve. For Parsifal, the work of the serpent is to heal the wounded masculine: to embody a new, more enlightened masculinity by integrating his inner feminine—qualities like beauty, feeling, and love that in most men lie dormant and must be actively awakened.

Central to the Parsifal legend is the Holy Grail, the chalice of Christ. The embodiment of the healing feminine, the Grail is the object of Parsifal's quest.

According to the legend, Parsifal—whose name means *innocent fool*—was an infant when his father died. He was raised by his mother in the forests of Wales, sheltered from men and their warrior ways. But in adolescence, he saw a group of knights riding through the woods. With their shining armor and flying banners, they were irresistible to the lad. The urge to become a man and prove his mettle stirred within him, and Parsifal decided to follow the knights on the quest for the Grail.

Parsifal's mother was distraught at the prospect of losing her son. She wanted him to remain forever her boy, safe by her side at home. She knew well that if he became a knight, he would lead a life of conflict, battling enemies in distant lands. "If you must go," she told him, "promise that you will remain chaste and will ask no questions, and that you will always wear this homespun shirt to remind you of your mother and her steadfast love." Being a dutiful son, Parsifal agreed to those conditions. When we're young, we follow the directives of our parents and the dictates of our culture, unaware of how constricting those prescribed roles might come to be in time.

Parsifal set off to find the knights, accepting the challenge to seek the Holy Grail. Soon after leaving the forest, Parsifal came upon the maiden Blanchefleur, or "white flower," who was preparing a wedding feast. Blanchefleur represents the pure feminine energy that exists within everyone, male or female; Parsifal must claim his inner lover if he is to become a whole man. But with his mother's words ringing in his ears, Parsifal upheld his vow of chastity and refused to marry Blanchefleur, instead choosing the life of the warrior. Even today, our young men are initiated by war, not love.

Continuing on his quest, Parsifal encountered the Red Knight, who had just come from King Arthur's court where he had overpowered everyone. When Parsifal asked how he, too, could become a knight, the Red Knight sent him to King Arthur. No one at court took Parsifal seriously, and when he asked for a horse and the armor of the Red Knight, Arthur smiled. "If you can defeat the Red Knight," he told Parsifal, "the horse and armor are yours." To everyone's astonishment, Parsifal not only challenged the Red Knight but won the duel, killing him. This awakened the virile warrior in Parsifal, but behind the swagger, his masculinity was not yet fully formed. Under his armor, he still wore his mother's homespun shirt.

Setting out again, Parsifal came to a castle that turned out to be where the Holy Grail was under the protection of the legendary Fisher King. Wounded in his groin—some versions say because he misused his sexual powers—the Fisher King represents the man whose masculinity is incomplete. Because the king was unable to procreate, his land was barren and his subjects were discontent. This is the condition of the modern male who has not been healed by the sacred Grail, initiated by love. He may work hard to make his family happy, yet he is powerless to do so, and feels unappreciated and unloved.

The Fisher King gave Parsifal the Grail Sword. The sword represents the masculine principle, charged with guarding the Holy Grail, the feminine force. The Fisher King hosted a feast, and at the end of the meal the Holy Grail was brought out. Everyone watched anxiously, for the legend said it would take an innocent young man to ask the question—"Whom does the Grail serve?"—that would release the Grail's power, the elixir that heals all wounds. Alas, when the cup was passed to Parsifal, he didn't recognize it as the Grail. Heeding his mother's plea not to ask questions, he simply passed the cup along. To his uninitiated mind, the vessel was just another cup of wine.

Parsifal woke the next day to find the castle empty and his horse saddled outside. As he rode across the drawbridge, the Grail castle disappeared into the mist behind him. Parsifal went on to rescue damsels in distress and liberate castles under siege, proving his worth as a knight performing the usual heroic deeds. At King Arthur's castle, the Knights of the Round Table welcomed him. But as they were celebrating Parsifal's triumphs, a crone interrupted the revelry. The old woman scolded Parsifal for failing to ask the Grail question, thereby losing the opportunity to release its healing power for the benefit of all mankind. Chastened and ridiculed by the old woman, Parsifal set off to find the Grail castle again and rectify his error. But he wandered for years without success, like many men who cannot find a deep and abiding love or a sense of fulfillment.

Finally, in old age, Parsifal met a group of travelers who berated him for wearing his armor on Good Friday, a holy day. The knight removed his armor, and with that he immediately received directions back to the Grail castle. There, at last—or so we hope, because the story ends before the conclusion—Parsifal posed the magic question, breaking the spell that had kept his masculinity wounded like the Fisher King's. Drinking from the vessel of pure, healing, feminine power, Parsifal became whole. It is only when a man sheds his armor, his warrior persona, that he can drink from the Grail cup and be healed by the Divine Feminine.

The Holy Grail is what all of us are searching for, men and women alike. The elixir it contains can soothe the wounds inflicted upon us by our violent, male-dominated history and the dictates of our parents and our culture. Like Parsifal, many of us don armor—a business suit, or a tough attitude, for example—and head off to battle each morning, freeing castles under siege but receiving no gratitude or satisfaction for our efforts.

As long as Parsifal remained tethered to the past and his identity as a warrior, he couldn't evolve into the man he was meant to be. He couldn't fulfill his promise to retrieve the Grail, so the people of the land suffered. Male or female, when we finally let go of who we think we're supposed to be and shed our fear of disapproval, we open our eyes to the new opportunities we encounter. We're no longer afraid to be curious, to ask questions, to take risks. But first we have to take off our armor and shed the homespun mother-garment underneath.

It's daunting to walk away from familiar issues and battles—to put down the sword and remove the emotional armor—but it's a crucial step in our evolution. Without taking this step, we will not recognize the Grail and release its healing power.

We may not even realize that we're holding on to the role of the misunderstood, underappreciated warrior, continuing to blame our parents for opportunities we didn't have and what we failed to become. But to break out of this victim identity, we have to recognize that our parents, too, lived the Parsifal myth, as did their parents and the generations before them. The journey of the healer involves breaking the chains of blame and stepping into a new role, writing a new story to free not only ourselves but also future generations.

Throughout our lives, we will continue to shed identities when, like the serpent's skin, they become too tight. Eventually we will discover that all roles are simply suits we hang in the closet, to put on and take off as circumstances require.

If you've done the work of the South and found your personal Grail, you're free to be the dreamer instead of the dreamed, the healer instead of the healed, the creator instead of the passive recipient of your life. Upon completing the healer's journey, you will find yourself facing in a new direction on the medicine wheel: West, the way of the jaguar.

EXERCISE
BURNING OLD ROLES AND IDENTITIES

The micro-fire ceremony is an effective practice for rewiring the brain and shedding outworn roles and identities so you can release the constraints of the past and move on. Like all shamanic practices, it requires focusing your intent on the task. Otherwise the ceremony won't have nearly as much depth or significance or transformative power.

Traditionally, this ceremony involves a group of people gathered around a large fire outdoors, but it can be just as meaningful as a solo rite indoors.

You will need a fat candle at least four inches tall, a box of wooden toothpicks, matches, and a fireproof bowl. (You can fill the bowl partway with sand, if you like.)

Light the candle, then take a toothpick, and as you hold it, think of a role or identity that is no longer serving you. Blow gently on the toothpick, envisioning that you are transferring all the energy of that outmoded role or identity into that small piece of wood. Then hold the toothpick to the candle flame. When you can no longer comfortably hang on to the flaming stick, drop it into the bowl. Continue blowing roles and identities into the toothpicks, one by one, until you have burned up all the stale old roles and identities you need to release.

The first time I did this exercise, I began with the role of *father.* As I brought the stick to the fire, I thanked my father for the love and lessons I had received from him, no matter how flawed they were. I know now that he did his best. I continued the ritual by releasing the role of *son,* and with a prayer, thanked my children for teaching me how to be a son and father. Then I moved on to shedding the identities of *husband, lover, healer, victim,* and so on, until I had burned up nearly 200 roles and identities! I hope you will have considerably fewer to burn.

THE JOURNEY TO THE DIVINE FEMININE:

FACING THE FEAR OF DEATH AND MEETING THE GODDESS

*Now on a certain day, while Mary stood near the
fountain to fill her pitcher, the angel of the Lord appeared
unto her, saying, "Blessed art thou, Mary, for in thy womb
thou hast prepared a habitation for the Lord. Behold,
light from heaven shall come and dwell in thee,
and through thee shall shine in all the world."*

—THE GOSPEL OF PSEUDO-MATTHEW

The Divine Mother, the symbol of the feminine, is found in all cultures, manifesting as the Madonna or Kali or Quan Yin—even as wisdom itself, the mother of all Buddhas. The shaman seeks to meet the Divine Feminine in her own domain—the rich, dark, inner world that we journey to when we face our fear of death. This journey is associated with the West direction on the medicine wheel, the place of the dying sun.

When we meet the Divine Feminine in the ordinary world, we are smitten. A man sees the goddess in the woman he falls in love with—until she begins to make his life impossible. When women meet the Divine Feminine in the world, they often idolize or envy her, instead of recognizing her beauty and power within themselves.

The Greek tale of the athlete Actaeon and Diana, goddess of the hunt and the moon, illustrates what can happen when we unexpectedly encounter the Divine Feminine. During a hunt with his hounds and his male friends, Actaeon left his companions resting and wandered off to explore a part of the forest he had never seen. He came upon a valley thick with pines and cypress, and a pristine stream that flowed into a shallow pool. There, to his surprise and delight, was the beautiful Diana, standing naked as her nymphs bathed her. The goddess had left her spear and bow and quiver of arrows on the riverbank beside her sandals and robe. When the nymphs saw Actaeon they quickly rushed to cover Diana with their own naked bodies, trying to hide the divine form from the young mortal's lustful gaze. But the goddess towered above her nymphs, and she stood proud, revealing her full body to the hunter. Splashing water in his face, she told him, "Now you can say you have seen Diana naked."

With that, antlers suddenly sprang from Actaeon's head; his muscular neck grew longer and sprouted fur; his arms turned into legs and his hands into hooves. Stunned, he bounded away, astonished at how quickly he could run. But when he stopped breathless by a pool and stooped to drink he caught his reflection in the water and saw that he had become a stag. At that instant he heard his own dogs baying and barking, hot on his trail. Terrified, he fled, but the dogs were soon at his heels, the first of them tearing at his flank. Actaeon tried calling their names, but only a strange, guttural sound came out of his mouth. In an instant the dogs felled him, ripping open his underbelly and tearing out his organs, as he bled to death.

In turning the lustful Actaeon into a stag, the symbol of male virility and power, the goddess transforms him into man's wildest fantasy—the all-fertile stud, the human horned god. In ancient Paleolithic art, shamans were portrayed as horned beings, like "The Sorcerer" in the famed cave painting at Trois-Frères in Ariège, France. Even today, we refer to all-male gatherings as stag parties. Meanwhile, the goddess is portrayed as granting all wishes—even our deepest, most unconscious ones, which, if we're not careful, may also contain the elements of our demise.

MEETING THE JAGUAR

The sun sets in the West, bringing forth the cacophony of night in the jungle. In the darkness, a sleek black cat moves silently. For the shaman, the jaguar is a potent symbol of the Divine Feminine. With no predators in the rain forest, the jaguar lives free of fear, taking just what it needs from the jungle for nourishment and no more. It doesn't kill out of greed, or for sport, or out of concern that the food supply will dry up. It doesn't scramble to be more, do more, or accomplish more. It doesn't need to prove itself. The jaguar hunts, explores, and sleeps as required, living a secure and balanced life.

To indigenous peoples in the southwestern United States, the Mexican jungles, and the Andean highlands, the jaguar represents the healing power of One Spirit Medicine in much the same way that the caduceus—the staff with two intertwined serpents crowned by eagle wings—symbolizes healing to Western physicians. In fact, the earliest civilization in the Americas, that of the Olmec of Mexico, was so fascinated with the jaguar that this great feline is depicted in much of Olmec art, including many figures that are half-human, half-jaguar.

For the Maya, the jaguar is a symbol of death and acceptance of death's role in the cycle of life. Before the Spanish conquest, the Mayan high priests were called balams—*balam* is Maya for jaguar—indicating they had traveled through the domains beyond death. They had made the symbolic journey to the underworld, conquered their fear of death, and returned with the elixir of immortality. In our journey to the Divine Feminine, we embody the wisdom of the jaguar, letting go of our fear of the unknown and trusting that what is dying inside us needs to be renewed in order to serve all life. With the cycle of life and death, harmony is reestablished. All species flourish as part of the balance of nature.

For us, the promise of the jaguar is to feel at home and safe regardless of any danger that surrounds us, and to live free of chronic disease. Doing the work of the jaguar, we discover that life provides us with everything we need. Jaguar gives us the confidence to step out and boldly explore, sure that we're headed where we need to go and that we're moving in synch with our life's purpose. Jaguar energy brings us into balance and sanity even if the world around us has gone mad, or we're paralyzed with fear and confusion, or we're faced with the prospect of debilitating disease. Jaguar returns our power and confidence, and restores our health. And if you allow jaguar to guide you far enough, she will lead you to the realm of the goddess to receive her wisdom directly.

If we complete this step on the medicine wheel, meeting the goddess and facing the fear of death, we can become like the jaguar, living with creativity and grace and experiencing wellness and balance. We can even hope to defeat death, like the ancient Mayan wisdom keepers, and discover our eternal nature.

To understand this concept of defeating death we need to consider the philosophy of the ancient Americans. They believed, as many people still do, that we have an essence that continues beyond death. But contrary to our Western religious thinking, in which the eternal nature of the soul is assumed, the shamans of old held that immortality is merely a seed, a potential that we all possess but one we have to awaken and empower to ensure the continuity of our consciousness beyond death. Our entire life, therefore, must be dedicated to spiritual practice, so that we can learn how to "leave this life alive," as the Amazon shamans say. The Maya called this process *the awakening of your jaguar body,* and the balams, the priests who had mastered it, were their prophecy keepers. The Tibetan Buddhist equivalent of the jaguar body is the light body. One effect of completing the work of the medicine wheel is to germinate the seeds of immortality you carry inside you.

DISCOVERING YOUR MORTALITY

Do you remember the first time you thought about your own death? The first time you faced the fact that you will die? In adolescence we feel impervious to death, believing it's something that happens to others but will never happen to us. And so, after one too many beers we drive down winding mountain roads with a carful of friends, denying that the laws of physics apply to us as we careen around the curves without giving safety a second thought. And then one day we lose a loved one or have an accident or a health scare, and we face the fact that death has always been by our side.

Actually, we have *two* great awakenings about mortality. The first is the one that occurs when we grasp that we're temporal beings and that one day our time on earth will end. If we take this awareness to heart, from that moment on we know that every moment is precious, and our lives are forever changed.

The second great awakening happens when we *master* our fear of death. This is the understanding that our nature is transtemporal—outside of time—and undying, continuing for all eternity. Our understanding of our eternal nature cannot be merely an intellectual one. It must be a visceral awareness, a knowing at a cellular level. In many preagricultural societies, there is a rite of initiation to foster this awareness, a symbolic encounter with death in which the initiate experiences the seamless continuity of life beyond physical existence.

Whether or not you consciously invite death in a rite of initiation, mastering the fear of death is immensely liberating, freeing you to use your creative faculties to find harmony in the chaos of everyday existence. The cacophony of the jungle becomes music. A tragedy becomes the foundation of a new and more fulfilling way of living. You start to envision a more enriching life for yourself and a more sustainable future for your community. You are called to serve the earth and all living beings, as you realize that we will continue together for eons to come.

After you've done the work of the jaguar, the new stories you write for yourself will be empowering and invigorating, extending beyond mere concern for your immediate needs. But be warned: If you try to rush the process by pushing aside your fear of death without acknowledging it, or scrambling to figure your way out of danger as quickly as possible, the initiation will be incomplete. The close brush with death will seem like a lucky break, not an invitation to discover your undying nature. The problems you thought you had left behind will in all likelihood return, as you slip into fear-based behaviors of the past. When the challenge of the jaguar remains unmet, life again becomes overwhelming, with no time left for the really important things.

To master fear, we need to return it to its rightful role as nature's early warning system, not as a habitual state of being. Fear alerts us to possible danger in our surroundings, making us ready to respond appropriately. But when fear settles into the nervous system instead of passing through it, we become possessed by it. The HPA axis goes into hyperdrive. Life turns chaotic at every level.

From the standpoint of biology, health is determined by the degree of harmony and complexity in the body. Nature favors complexity. The human being evolved from a single-celled organism into a highly specialized creature. But complexity alone is not enough to create health; the system must be coherent and harmonious as well. A hundred people playing a hundred different musical instruments do not make an orchestra. To create music these instruments have to play in harmony.

The more complex and coherent the systems in your body, the healthier you will be. Heart rate variability—naturally occurring fluctuations in the rhythm of the heartbeat—is one measure of overall health. The more variable your heart rate, the healthier your heart, and the more harmoniously all the systems in your body work together, the greater your resilience and health.

This understanding of coherence and complexity is reflected even in health at the cellular level. Orderly cells create health, while disorderly cells revert back to a primitive state and begin to form tumors. Chaotic cells steal nourishment from the body and unlike healthy cells, refuse to die. They defy the instructions of the mitochondria—the structures in the cells that control the cells' "death clock"— to die off so that younger, more vital cells can replace them. When cells lose their complexity, they can no longer feed on healthy fats but only on sugars—which is why eliminating all sugars and carbohydrates from your diet is so important for healing from cancer and other diseases.[1]

As cancerous cells multiply in the body, they wreak havoc, ultimately killing the host that is feeding them. And what happens at a cellular level is reflected in what happens to your life if you refuse to accept endings as a natural part of life. When fear of death takes over, it determines what your experiences will be, eventually sucking the life out of you.

ENDINGS, TRANSITIONS, AND BEGINNINGS

We have to let ourselves be terrified by the transition that death of the old ushers in. Fear of death—whether death of the body, a way of thinking, a relationship, a situation, or a dream—has to be experienced fully and consciously, and then overcome for new, healthy growth to take place.

At just 12 years old, Annie was the youngest cancer patient I had ever worked with. Her parents had brought her to see me in the hope that One Spirit Medicine would reverse her brain cancer. They had tried every conceivable medical intervention to no avail and were looking to me for the cure they had failed to find anywhere else. Annie had lost all her hair from chemotherapy and looked like a young, smiling Buddha as she sat in a big leather chair in my office.

I explained to Annie's parents the difference between healing and curing. While curing is the elimination of symptoms, healing works at a much deeper level, treating the causes of the imbalance that lead to disease. And while a cure is the ideal outcome of a medical intervention, healing is the product of a journey in which all aspects of your life are transformed—even if you end up dying. You carry your healed self into your next life.

I asked Annie's parents to sit outside in the waiting area so I could be alone with her. After a few moments of small talk, she told me bluntly, "I'm not afraid." She went on to say that angels came to her every night in her dreams—and even during the day at times. But her parents were deathly afraid for her. "I can't tell them about the angels," Annie said. But she thought I would understand. And I did. I sensed that the veils between the worlds were parting for Annie and that her spirit was preparing for the great journey home. But her parents were understandably determined to do everything possible to help Annie live, and this meant trying to get rid of her cancer by taking her to a string of specialists and finally, as a last resort, to me.

I've been a practicing shaman long enough to understand that death is part of life. And I have seen that some of my most successful healings consisted of helping my clients die peacefully and consciously. So I performed an Illumination on Annie, to help bring balance to her energy field and thus to her body. The Illumination is the core healing practice of shamanic energy medicine, in which the luminous energy field is cleared of the imprints of disease to help mobilize the body's own healing systems.

Annie's doctors had not given her long to live. But I know that death is a doorway to continued life in the world of Spirit. I worked on Annie's chakras, clearing them of the heavy energies that had accumulated in them, helping to lighten her energetic load for the great journey ahead of her. As she lay on my treatment table, she went into a deep sleep, although her body twitched as she released energies bound up in her chakras.

At the end of our session, Annie returned to the leather chair that almost seemed to swallow her, a smile on her face. "Am I going to be okay?" she asked me, and we both knew what she was talking about. I had sensed the angels in the room as I did the Illumination. "Yes," I said. "You're going to be just fine." And then she asked me how she could help her mother and father. "They're really afraid," she said. I'm always stunned by the wisdom of so many children—and equally stunned by the lack of wisdom in so many adults.

When Annie's parents came back into the room, they found both of us smiling. I told them what great work their daughter had done. I suggested they eliminate all gluten from Annie's diet, as well as sugar, dairy, and all possible allergens. Then I recommended that she take omega-3 fatty acids daily to help rebuild the regions in the brain that had been damaged by chemo. At no time is it more important to have your brain whole than when you are coming to the end of your life. The neural apparatus has to be in the best working order possible for you to pass consciously into the world of Spirit.

I learned that Annie passed away a few months later with a smile on her face, in the arms of her angels.

LOVE AND LETTING GO

The forest undergrowth and canopy can't grow unless the soil is replenished by the decaying bodies of dead plants. Even the jaguar will die, feeding the tree that will feed the monkey that the next jaguar will feast on. The balance of life in the forest wouldn't be possible without death, just as we can't live in a state of harmony with our environment unless endings are a part of our lives.

Things have to die for new things to be born. Death and life are always in balance.

The work of the jaguar helps us find a balance between, on the one hand, engaging life aggressively and seizing opportunity at all costs and, on the other, approaching life with acceptance and receptivity so we can surrender to the larger creative process. It's a delicate dance between masculine, aggressive energy and feminine, receptive energy. The jaguar teaches us that we can stop hoarding, stop taking more than we need, because Mother Earth will provide us with plenty. We can trust that what lies ahead around a blind corner may actually be better than what we see now.

The work of the jaguar allows us to stop grasping at the past and start living more optimistically and imaginatively. Then, instead of worrying about the sun setting, we can enjoy the evening stars and look forward to the sun rising again at just the right time. The obsession with losing what we have—our youth, our belongings, our loved ones, our health—begins to fade. Our relationship with death becomes a healthy one.

Entropy is the law of physics that says that everything in the universe is moving toward chaos and disorder, toward breakdown and death. Temporary disorder and disorientation are necessary preludes to reorganization at a higher level. This is what we experience when we begin a new relationship, a new career, or a new health plan. Change holds danger but also the potential for something new—and better—to be born.

In the West on the medicine wheel, we come to terms with the cycle of destruction and rebirth, the natural order of the universe. We grasp at a deep level that creative chaos can lead to greater harmony and balance. In Hinduism, the cycle of destruction and rebirth is represented by the Trimurti, the three principal deities controlling the cosmos: Brahma the creator, Vishnu the preserver, and Shiva the destroyer.

Once we face our fear and experience the sense of loss and despair in every bone in our body, no longer denying it or running away from it, the fear dissipates. Then we can immerse ourselves in the chaos of creation, the primordial soup from which new life arises. There is no dipping a toe into the pool cautiously; total immersion is the only way to experience full initiation into a new stage of being and perceiving. Allowing ourselves to be truly terrified by the unknown, we can let go of the safety of the shore and plunge into unfamiliar waters, aware of the risks but excited by the possibilities.

Many of us hesitate to surrender fully to loving another because we fear losing the loved one. In my late 20s, after suffering what I called chronic heartbreak, I vowed never again to be involved in a deeply committed love relationship. The pain of losing the person I was so deeply attached to was too great to bear. And then, after a couple of emotionally barren years, I realized how futile my vow was. Love can't be guaranteed. One day, after reading a poem of Rumi's, I decided to face my fear. Rumi said to his beloved, "For I have ceased to exist, only you are here." This was the complete opposite of what I had sought in all my earlier relationships. My mantra then was, "For you have ceased to exist, only I am here." Gradually I began to understand, as Rumi did, that in reality all love is, at bottom, a longing for Spirit—for the true Beloved—and that my deepest fear was not of losing my partner but of never finding myself.

RETURN FROM THE UNDERWORLD

Overcoming the fear that holds us back from a new dream is a universal theme in mythology. Understanding mythic journeys of death and rebirth can help us with the work of the jaguar.

In Greek mythology, the underworld was a complex place filled with malevolent spirits, rivers with magical powers, and a queen who ruled the shadowy realm and knew its secrets. Among the mortals who, according to legend, entered the underworld alive and emerged unscathed was Hercules, who had the strength to overpower the three-headed guard dog Cerberus.

Courage and strength allowed Hercules to survive what seemed like a fatal mission. It takes courage to stay with fear and breathe into the emotion rather than run away from it or try to subdue it. But when courage becomes bravado, it can be our undoing, as it was for the musician Orpheus. After his wife, Eurydice, died and was whisked away to Hades, Orpheus descended to the underworld in pursuit. There, with his sweet music, he persuaded King Hades and Queen Persephone to allow Eurydice to return to the land of the living. But just as they reached the threshold, Orpheus, disobeying Hades, glanced back at his beloved. With that, she was banished to the shadowy realm forever. Orpheus survived, but his love was forever lost.

PSYCHE AND HER JOURNEY TO THE UNDERWORLD

To meet the healing power of the Divine Feminine, we can look to another mortal, Psyche, who descended to the underworld and survived. Psyche is the Greek word for *soul,* and her story describes the journey that everyone, male or female, must take if they seek to defeat death and be initiated by love.

The youngest and loveliest daughter of a king, Psyche was so beloved by everyone that Aphrodite, goddess of love, became jealous and drove all of Psyche's suitors away. The king consulted an oracle, who told him that he must chain his daughter to a rock to be courted by and married to Death, a horrible monster. The myth tells us that the young, innocent part of ourselves—full of fresh ideas and the changes they bring—threatens the old ways. Psyche's challenge was to face Death, and she did, but not in the way she thought she would.

Aphrodite sent her son Eros to shoot an arrow of love into Psyche so that the maiden would be irresistibly attracted to Death. But just as Eros was about to carry out his mother's wishes, he became so distracted by Psyche's beauty that he pricked himself with one of his own arrows and fell in love with her himself. He swept Psyche away to his home in the mountains, defying the threats of his mother, who believed that Psyche's beauty and vitality must be destroyed. As the myth points out, this is precisely what fear of death and loss can do—destroy our beauty and vitality.

Eros was kind and loving to Psyche with one caveat: she was never to look at him. Not wanting to reveal he was a god, he came to her only after dark. Psyche agreed to the conditions and delighted in her unseen husband. But when her sisters came to visit, envious of Psyche's good fortune, they persuaded her to disobey her husband's orders. "What if he's a monster?" they asked.

Psyche hadn't been afraid of the unknown before, but after her sisters' warning, fear got the better of her. She went to sleep with a plan, and after making love to her husband, quickly lit a lamp so she could see his face and form. She discovered the beautiful Eros sleeping sweetly and was overjoyed to see he wasn't a monster after all. But then, a drop of hot oil from the lamp fell on Eros's shoulder, and he woke up. Furious that Psyche had disobeyed him, he flew away. In giving in to her own fear amid social pressure from her sisters, she destroyed her happy life.

Psyche entreated the gods for help, but they all feared Aphrodite. In fact, gods are no help in a situation like this, for they are bound to tradition and the old ways. The gods told the devastated Psyche that the only way she could right the situation was to get into Aphrodite's good graces. Though terrified, Psyche took their advice and bravely approached her mother-in-law. She was ready for the work of the West: confronting and overcoming her fears.

Aphrodite, however, was furious that Psyche had dared to approach her. The goddess took the young woman by the hair and smashed her head against the ground. She then assigned Psyche four impossible tasks she had to complete if she wanted her husband back. The first was to sort a huge pile of seeds before nightfall; if Psyche failed, she would die. This task represents our fear of time running out. *How will we have time to accomplish everything in our lives? How can we sort what's important from what isn't? Will we have enough time for the things that really matter to us?* With the help of a colony of ants, Psyche managed to complete the task. The ants represent the assistance that is always available to us if we look. None of us can do the seemingly impossible alone.

Psyche's second task was to cross a river and retrieve the fleece from the fierce magical rams grazing in a field. The rams represent our fear of adversaries more powerful than we are. We all have to face these adversaries in the form of bosses and family and other obligations in life. Once again, Psyche completed the task with help. The reeds growing on the riverbank told her to wait until dusk when the rams fell asleep; then she could collect the fleece that had stuck to the reeds when the rams rubbed against them, without risking discovery by the sheep. By allowing the situation to resolve itself, Psyche freed herself from the need to take on an enemy who would easily overpower her.

The third task was to fill a crystal goblet with water from the source of the River Styx, a sacred spring high on a mountain that was protected by sleepless dragons. This was an impossible task for a mortal. Even the gods would be leery of such an assignment. In the course of our lives, we all face seemingly impossible tasks. And when we fear we're not smart enough, good enough, strong enough, or brave enough to handle them, we're like Psyche facing the unattainable. She despaired until an eagle appeared, took the goblet in its talons, flew to the mountaintop, filled the goblet with water from the sacred spring, and brought it back to her, helping her accomplish the superhuman task. The eagle, soaring high in the sky, represents the overarching vision, the attention to the big picture, that is necessary to overcome our fears, coupled with the daring to go where ordinary birds would never fly. In the same way, the promise of One Spirit Medicine can help us overcome our fear of facing uncertainty and aiming high, as we undergo the process of initiation. Like the ants and reeds, the eagle represents the helpful forces the universe provides, the synchronous events that occur in our lives when we have the courage to take risks despite our fear.

Psyche's fourth task was to descend into the underworld and ask Persephone for some of her precious beauty cream to give Aphrodite. Frightened beyond words, Psyche decided to take her own life, a guaranteed one-way ticket to the realm of the dead. She climbed an abandoned stone tower and was just about to jump when the tower told her where to find the entrance to the underworld, advising her to carry two coins and two barley cakes with her, and to neither accept assistance from any shades she met in the underworld nor give assistance to anyone who asked her for it. This is the most valuable advice anyone can give us on a journey to conquer fear. We must bring gifts—our abilities and strengths, and qualities like generosity and compassion—and we must be careful who we ask to help us. Even friends who have our best interests at heart often can't or won't provide the assistance or advice we need. Although tempted to help the shades who cried out to her, Psyche followed orders and ignored their pleas. She paid Charon the ferryman, fed the guard dog Cerberus, and accepted only a snack, not a banquet, from Persephone. At last, she successfully retrieved the jar of beauty cream for Aphrodite. Despite her natural urge to help others, Psyche stayed on task, just as we have to focus on our own initiation and not allow ourselves to be diverted by other people's needs as a way of avoiding the inner work we must do.

Psyche was on the verge of successfully completing her tasks, when, like Orpheus, she gave in to temptation. She peeked inside the jar she was carrying and instantly fell asleep. In her impatience, she tried to rush the process of initiation, and as a result, slipped back into an unawakened state. Her folly serves as a cautionary tale as we complete the lessons of the jaguar. In older versions of the myth Psyche returned to the world with the beauty cream intact, but the gods became jealous and took it away, then granted her immortality to keep her from sharing the secret of eternal youth with other humans. In another version, however, all was not lost: Psyche was rescued by Eros—the force of romantic and sexual love, which has the power to restore life. As for Aphrodite, she had known all along that Psyche would open the jar, which contained not beauty cream but the elixir of immortality. Psyche's deep sleep represents the death of her old, limited sense of self. Then when she awakened, she was granted immortality by Zeus.

For us what is most significant about Psyche's tale is her initiation in the underworld. She has to face her fear of death so she can transform her life.

All initiation involves a journey to the realm of death and a meeting with the Divine Feminine from which you return renewed. This isn't like the superficial change that comes from making minor tweaks in your life. The journey to the Divine Feminine, like Parsifal's quest for the Grail, is demanding. You have to endure the fear of going to the underworld and remaining there in deep reflection before you can emerge to light and clarity. If you think what you bring back is just salve for your wounds, you miss the point. The cream isn't ordinary wrinkle cream—or a souvenir on par with a T-shirt or tote bag printed with the slogan, *I went to Hades and back!* The beauty cream brings rejuvenation and reinvention. The elixir of immortality is the prize for completing the work of the West.

There is no rushing the journey of initiation. Mastering the fear of death is a lifelong process. You may be challenged and tested many times, although with each time, the way becomes easier.

Once you have reclaimed the ability to reinvent yourself, you're ready for the next direction on the medicine wheel, the North. There, you will learn to become still, so you can retrieve lost aspects of your soul.

MEDITATE WITH JAGUAR

Jaguars are masters of meditation. Have you ever watched a cat lounging in the sun? Cats know perfect relaxation. A jaguar in the rain forest perches on the lower branches of a tree and watches the world go by, undisturbed by the monkeys and the macaws, completely at ease yet totally alert, with only the tip of its tail twitching now and then. The jaguar teaches us how to relax. Deeply relax. (Try explaining to your cat that there are important things to worry about.)

Today we understand that much of the imbalance in our bodies is caused by our inability to slow down and release tension. Our sympathetic nervous system is designed to provide us with the reflexes to fight or flee when we're in danger. And when the system is switched on, we can't relax for even a few seconds. Cortisol and adrenaline flood the bloodstream to give us a burst of energy to deal with threats. But these powerful chemicals are not meant to course through the body for more than a short time. If we're truly in danger, we fight or flee and then quickly recover, as the adrenaline and cortisol are reabsorbed into the body's system and our breathing slows to normal. But when we're chronically on high alert, paralyzed with anxiety, toxic levels of cortisol remain in the body, causing inflammation and neuron damage and, ultimately, disease. Instead of mastering our fear of death, our fear of death masters us. Our jaguar has climbed to the uppermost branches of the tree like a terrified kitten—and we're powerless to call the fire department to bring it down.

All of us will die someday; however, we don't have to experience the slide to death prematurely. We can master our fear of death so that our lives are not dictated by dread and we are not constantly responding as if a jungle beast were poised to pounce on us at any minute. We can return to a balanced, calm, relaxed state, switching on our parasympathetic nervous system so the pineal gland can produce the spirit molecules, and be graceful jaguars, savoring our newly discovered visceral wisdom about the infinite nature of life.

CHAPTER 11

THE JOURNEY OF THE SAGE:

BECOMING STILL IN MIDAIR

[Behold] many wonders that no one has ever seen before . . .
Behold here today . . . the whole universe, of the moving
and the unmoving, and whatever else you may desire
to see, all concentrated in My body . . . But with these
eyes of yours you cannot see Me. I give you a divine
eye; behold, now, my sovereign yoga-power.

—BHAGAVAD GITA

When the ancestors of the native peoples of the Americas migrated from Asia more than 30,000 years ago, they brought with them a body of wisdom from their long residence in the foothills of the Himalayas. According to molecular archeologists who track variations of mitochondrial DNA, a dozen or so courageous travelers crossed the great Siberian plains to Beringia, a land mass that covered what is now the Bering Strait between Russia and Alaska. They then descended through North and Central America to the Andes, and from there all the way down to Tierra del Fuego, at the tip of South America. Along the way they built cliff dwellings and citadels among the clouds, like Machu Picchu. In Andean mythology, therefore, the North is the direction of the ancestors. The way of the sage is associated with the North on the medicine wheel and with age-old practices of stillness.

The North is not just the direction of the great sages of the past and our biological forebears but also where we experience calm in the midst of furious activity. The North Star is the only still point in a moving sky. And in Native American mythology, North is associated with the hummingbird, which appears to be perfectly still even as it beats its wings rapidly to remain suspended in midair. Some species of hummingbirds migrate from Canada to South America every fall, flying thousands of miles over the vast ocean. So from the hummingbird we also learn that with stillness comes the ability to go boldly into uncharted territory and make our lives an epic journey regardless of how many oceans we have to cross.

The way of the sage hones our ability to transcend the restless activity of the mind obsessed with the challenges, dramas, and mundane details of life and remain at peace with whatever is happening within and around us. We begin to see order at the heart of uncertainty and tranquility in the eye of the storm. Abandoning fixed ideas about how things should be, we instead take delight in watching plans manifest and dissolve in kaleidoscopic fashion, arranged and rearranged by the vagaries of everyday life. It is in the North that we learn to embrace the Yiddish proverb, "Man plans, God laughs."

The newfound sense of inner peace that arises as we complete the work of the sage is the direct result of a radical shift in awareness. Only when we've stopped grasping and yearning, avoiding and worrying, endeavoring, and battling can we find equanimity. In stillness, we can access the wisdom of the ancestors. This is the wisdom that Psyche retrieved from Persephone, knowledge we acquire only in the non-ordinary world, where we experience eternity in every cell of our being. The gift of the North is stillness in motion.

From the perspective of neuroscience, the wisdom of the North is associated with the neocortex, which allowed us to survive without the teeth and claws of stronger, more nimble animals, and later to discover the wonders of science, sending the Hubble Space Telescope into orbit and positing string theory to explain what the universe is made of. Packed into the dense neural networks of the neocortex are regions for language, attention, and self-awareness as well as appreciation of beauty and the ability to make art. The neocortex first revealed its gifts around 50,000 years ago, when our ancestors began to paint their mystical representations of their world on the walls of caves at Lascaux in France and Altamira in Spain. However, the rational capacity of the neocortex, if used unwisely, can also be employed to make war and wreak havoc—destructive power that was probably unleashed shortly after *Homo sapiens* discovered cave painting, as we eliminated our Neanderthal cousins.

But once we have tamed the warrior instinct during the journey of the healer in the South, the neocortex is free to support our higher instincts and aspirations. It moves us to feel joy, compassion, and empathy—sentiments that lift us beyond the lurid tales of who did what to whom that occupy the more primitive brain.

The gifts of the North are accessible to us when we stop and see that we've been going a hundred miles an hour yet getting nowhere, and doing a million things yet achieving nothing. Initially, the way of the sage in the North seems like the easiest direction on the medicine wheel to master, given the instructions: *Sit back! Relax! Enjoy the view!* But you can't get to the North without healing your masculine side in the South and journeying beyond death to meet the Divine Feminine in the West. And when you reach the North, you will most likely find that doing nothing is harder than it looks. And staying still is not an end in itself but the necessary ground, the fundamental practice, for witnessing the entirety of the universe and experiencing the vastness of creation. In the journey of the sage we acquire that divine eye that allows us to comprehend the entire nature of creation. But to acquire this form of vision requires stillness.

With our hectic lives today, being still feels next to impossible. We're so used to multitasking and tracking continual input from our digital devices that quieting the mind for more than a few seconds is a Herculean task. Even when we meditate, focusing on our breathing, we can't resist the urge to scratch an itch, adjust our posture, or curse ourselves for not turning off the text alert on our cell phones.

It is the nature of the mind to jump about, and the overactive mind has been the focus of meditation masters since ancient times. But our minds today are even more restless, flitting from topic to topic with the dizzying speed of jump cuts in an action film. But if you can slow the inner movie and quiet the internal racket, you will be able to access the vast reservoir of wisdom that is humanity's ancestral memory bank.

In the North we learn that what we call reality is an illusion, albeit one we are jointly re-creating in every instant—"What is reality anyway? Nothing but a collective hunch," as the comedian Lily Tomlin put it. We come to realize that the universe mirrors back to us perfectly our beliefs, our intentions, our sincerity. *What is* is the product of the map of reality you carry inside you. If you want to change your experience, you need to change the map.

Neuroscientists believe this map is embedded in the neural networks of the brain. Shamans believe it resides in the topography of the luminous energy field. But regardless of where your model of the world resides, to bring about change in your world you will need to upgrade the quality of your map—exchange the outmoded model for a better one. If, like so many of us in this culture, you are relying on a fear-ridden, scarcity-laden, violent map to navigate through life, to open yourself to the experience of One Spirit Medicine you will need to replace it with a vast and liberating map that includes the entire universe. This is what the warrior Arjuna discovers in his dialogue with the god Krishna, which forms the central narrative of the *Bhagavad Gita,* an ancient Hindu text.

ARJUNA: THE CHALLENGE TO BE STILL AND MEET GOD

The *Bhagavad Gita* was written at a time when the Indian subcontinent was rife with conflict between royal families. As the narrative begins, the archer Arjuna is preparing to do battle against a formidable army of his relatives. It is Arjuna's karma, his duty to fight, but he is deeply conflicted at the prospect of battling his own kin. War in this legend is a metaphor for the challenges involved in dealing with the conflicts of human existence, and Krishna, in his advice to Arjuna, imparts timeless wisdom for quieting the inner turmoil we all face. Only when we still the inner war can we receive the wisdom of the universe.

Arjuna cries out to Krishna, who is acting as his charioteer, to help him avoid the battle that will surely result in death and suffering for all. Just as both sides are about to charge, Krishna stops the action, like a director freezing the frame of an epic film just before the bloodshed begins. Like Arjuna, we find it almost impossible to gain any perspective on our lives when we're embroiled in a battle with our boss or spouse or children—even in a fight for our health—and we're trying to sort out what to do. We have to become still in the midst of the turmoil so we can observe clearly how our actions and the actions of others, past and present, fit together in the tapestry of life. In the timeless instant when we stop moving and simply witness the moment, the dust settles and the big picture emerges. Then, with this new map of reality in hand, we can choose wisely what course to pursue.

With both armies frozen in mid-motion, Krishna shows Arjuna how the illusions of the restless mind deceive us. Reflecting on this, Arjuna says:

The mind is restless, unsteady,
turbulent, wild, stubborn;
truly, it seems to me
as hard to master as the wind.[1]

Struggle is a part of life, Krishna tells Arjuna, but we have to resist getting caught up in the dramas we create around our struggles. Then we can take whatever action is necessary "without any thought of results, / open to success or failure."[2]

Our ordinary mental maps can help us figure out how to navigate everyday life, but there are times when their limitations are clear. Whenever our survival maps are running the show, our emotions and hard-core beliefs get in the way. When that happens, we need to stop and observe what is happening without judgment. In the stillness, we can hear a higher voice. Then we realize that Spirit has been with us all along, steering our chariot true, just as Krishna steers Arjuna's. Krishna tells Arjuna:

For the man who wishes to mature,
the yoga of action is the path;
for the man already mature,
serenity is the path.[3]

Like the hummingbird flying over the ocean in response to a distant calling, we can rely on our inner guidance to lead us safely to the other shore. Krishna explains to Arjuna that everything we do can become an offering to the divine and that we shouldn't be fixated on achieving specific results. Sometimes when we're pulled off course, it's because we're meant to experience something other than what we planned. Spirit may have ideas for our life that don't make sense to us at first. There is a greater order that is invisible to humans, Krishna tells Arjuna, and we have to align ourselves with this higher plan.

In stillness, we can receive as much guidance from Spirit as we are willing to invite. Sometimes all we want to know is how to respond to our lover or our child; other times we may be ready to learn the true nature of reality and the cosmos. We can set the bar at whatever level we want. We may be called to action or to nonaction. (Nonaction doesn't mean doing nothing but rather making a conscious choice not to intervene, allowing situations that can resolve themselves on their own to do so.) Not acting can be even more powerful than acting: it requires great strength not to make a move or react or rescue someone. Non-doing is the essential practice of the North. When we choose to refrain from action and remain still, the fabric of reality is revealed to us and we recognize its awesome precision.

Perceiving the hidden fabric of life is true wisdom. Knowing how we fit into the grand story of creating and weaving this fabric gives us the perspective of the sage. Like Arjuna, we experience the perfection of life, as we witness the vast domain of Spirit:

> Thou art the first of gods, the ancient Soul; Thou art the supreme Resting-place of the universe; Thou art the Knower and That which is to be known and the Ultimate Goal. And by Thee is the world pervaded, O Thou of infinite form. Thou art Wind and Death and Fire and Moon and the Lord of Water. Thou art the First Man and the Great-grandsire.[4]

Since most of us are unlikely to meet a Krishna, how can we witness the vast workings of creation? In the West we're more likely to look to science than to Spirit. The French anthropologist Claude Lévi-Strauss said that for us to know the workings of the universe, we first have to understand the workings of a blade of grass: how photosynthesis transforms light into life and how the roots of that blade of grass absorb minerals from the earth. An indigenous person, however, approaches the matter from a different perspective; for him to know the workings of a blade of grass, he first has to know intuitively the workings of the universe—how suns are created and how galaxies are formed. Today, maybe for the first time in history, we have the opportunity to do both.

One of the most effective ways of quieting manic mental activity and finding stillness is to pay attention to the space between breaths. It's in the pause—the moment between inhaling and exhaling—that you find stillness. Breathing is an autonomic response, and we can't stop it altogether or we die. But we can change the rate of respiration. Breathing practices, many of them ancient techniques, are designed to bring the mind into a state of tranquility and balance. We have the power to cultivate equanimity by consciously controlling the breath.

As you cultivate stillness, everyday challenges will cease to assume crisis proportions. When you're able to take a more expansive view, the world becomes a place of abundance that supports a rich and rewarding life. The frenetic race to get ahead gives way to an awareness that life doesn't have to be a struggle. In the North, you are called to bring beauty, healing, and peace to yourself and the world. How best to carry out this mission may not be immediately apparent, but as you continue to practice stillness, it will be revealed to you. All you need to do is make a commitment to healing and then let Spirit take care of the details. As Krishna explains to Arjuna:

> Those who take refuge in me,
> striving for release from old age
> and death, know absolute freedom,
> and the Self, and the nature of action.[5]

PILGRIMAGE: A JOURNEY OF THE NORTH

A few years ago, I met a woman, Chloe, who was engaged in a battle for her health. She chose to make a pilgrimage, a practice that was once commonplace, especially in Europe during the Middle Ages. Her pilgrimage was going to take her to northwestern Spain, where she planned to retrace the steps of the apostle Santiago—Saint James—who walked from the Mediterranean to Santiago de Compostela, a journey of some 500 miles.

A pilgrimage involves a geographical destination, and the Camino de Santiago, or Way of Saint James, has been popular for centuries among pilgrims who walk all or part of the route. But a pilgrimage is more than a trek through the countryside; it's also an inner journey, a time of self-reflection. Many pilgrims dedicate the journey to something larger than themselves. Chloe hoped her pilgrimage would give her a renewed sense of purpose and clarity that would allow her to meet the health challenges she faced.

Soon after she began her journey, Chloe thought she heard a faint voice telling her that she should fast for three days, drinking only water, and then eat for three days, alternating the two for the entire journey. By the time she arrived in Santiago de Compostela three months later, she had recovered her health. While she attributes her recovery to divine intervention, I'm sure that the fasting helped turn on all her body's repair systems. And the stillness and serenity she practiced allowed her to understand the lessons that her illness had brought her.

You don't need to walk the Camino de Santiago to reap the healing benefits of pilgrimage. You could turn your daily commute to work, or a visit to your estranged daughter, or like Chloe, the path back to wellness into a pilgrimage. Whatever the journey, it will have an outer component, with obstacles you have to surmount, and an inner component that involves surrender, discovery, and most likely emotional challenges, as you open yourself to redrawing your mental map with Spirit's help. Once you have clarity on the greater map for your life and your healing, you can take the necessary action to align yourself with the new direction.

In many indigenous cultures, the pilgrimage is traditionally a solitary vision quest. The seeker primes his brain with a combination of fasting and superfoods. Then he goes deep into the forest or another natural setting and opens to divine guidance.

The vision quest is the last, all-important step for receiving One Spirit Medicine, and you'll find instructions for setting up your own in Chapter 13. But first you must finish the journey around the medicine wheel and follow the path of the visionary in the East.

EXERCISE
I AM MY BREATH

Traditional practices for cultivating stillness and equanimity involve working with the breath. This basic exercise is effective for quieting the mind.

Sit quietly in a darkened room with a small, lighted candle before you. As you gaze at the candle, note that your awareness is like the flame, darting here and there, blown first in one direction and then another.

Invite your mind to be the observer as you focus on your in-breath. Find the space at the top of the breath where the lungs are comfortably full and pause there for an instant, silently repeating: *I am my breath.*

As you exhale, notice how your breath stirs the flame ever so slightly. Release all the air in your lungs, and at the bottom of the breath, pause for an instant and silently repeat: *I am my breath.*

Continue the exercise for five to ten minutes at first. As you become more comfortable sitting still, gradually increase the time.

CHAPTER 12

THE JOURNEY OF THE VISIONARY:

RECEIVING ONE SPIRIT MEDICINE

Listen to the hidden sounds.
Use your other ears.
See the celestial sights.
Use your other eyes.
Perceive what cannot be
measured by the ordinary senses.

On the medicine wheel, the journey of the visionary is associated with the East, the direction of rebirth, where the life-giving sun rises each morning, bringing us an opportunity to meet our world anew. Among indigenous peoples of the Americas, the East is the direction toward which the teepee or ceremonial lodge faces, allowing the power of the new dawn to warm and fill the space.

The East is represented by the eagle, which can soar high above the clouds, surveying the entire landscape, or home in on a mouse scurrying in the bushes. This dual perspective of both sky-level awareness and ground-level clarity is why the East is known as the way of the seer or the visionary. At this point in our journey we learn to put the cart before the horse; to look at the possibilities before acknowledging the dour probabilities or limitations; to focus on why something can be so, rather than why it cannot.

One gift of the eagle is the ability to start afresh, free of the old stories about who we are, unbounded by expectations or fears or doubts. Every gift from Spirit entails an obligation, however, and in the East the obligation is to share the wisdom you've acquired with others. Armed with a new, more expansive map for your life, you can stop thinking your way out of one mess and into another, and simply appreciate each moment in all its wonder.

This heightened level of awareness, in which you experience yourself as an inseparable part of the cosmos, is difficult to sustain. But even when you return to ordinary awareness, you bring with you the knowledge that you can transform your life at the deepest level by holding a vision of the possible. You can share this gift with others by inviting them to entertain their highest dreams, as you help them rise from their deepest nightmare. Every time a new patient walks into my office, I see the person as a healthy, luminous, and joyous being, regardless of the diagnosis they carry with them. I know that holding this healed image of my clients will help them discover their path to wellness. Only when I have this image firmly in mind do I start looking at where the person is hurting and what seems to be wrong.

It's in bringing others the healing gifts we've received that the benefits of these gifts become truly ours. In our Light Body School I train students to practice energy medicine, to become master shamans, and to bring beauty and healing to others and the world. The training begins with healing the notion of an "I" that is separate from other beings and the cosmos, and that is powerless and helpless. If you're still attached to a limited sense of self and scared to lose your identity as an individual, you will not be able to tolerate the experience of Oneness, the unity of One Spirit Medicine, or the gifts of power and grace that accompany it.

In the *Bhagavad Gita,* Krishna tells Arjuna, "I am immortality and I am also death personified. Both being and nonbeing are in me." You, I, and Spirit are being and nonbeing at once. You and I exist as independent entities only from the perspective of serpent, of the ordinary world.

This shift in awareness to the perspective of eagle allows you to become the dreamer instead of the dreamed. You come to grasp that everyone holds a piece of the cosmic puzzle, that you are not the only dreamer. You are collaborating with others and with Spirit to dream your health—and a healed and beautiful world—into being. Dreaming in this sense is going on all the time, whether or not you are aware of it. But in the journey of the visionary, you can choose to consciously participate in dreaming the world into being.

The recognition that dreaming is a collective endeavor frees you from the burden of thinking that you are the sole master of your universe but you're failing miserably at the job. At the same time, however, it allows you to own the power you *do* have to bring about change in your health and your relationships—indeed, in every aspect of your life. Armed with this awareness, you neither try to run away from crises nor are overwhelmed by them. You are able to see clearly when and how to take action, and when to let problems resolve themselves and the body heal on its own.

In the North, you developed the consciousness that allows you to observe your mind during the practice of stillness. Here in the East, you come to see that the consciousness that observes your experience is an inextricable part of a larger consciousness. To realize this, the Indian sage Ramana Maharshi used to recommend an exercise of self-inquiry to his students. You start by bringing your attention to the feeling of self, of *I,* and holding your attention there until the feeling of *I* disappears and only awareness remains. This is a difficult practice for most of us, so as an aid, you can begin with the practice I was taught by the shamans and used in my healing. Reflect on the question *Who am I?* then move on to *Who is it who is asking the question?*

This exploration will take you beyond the experience of the ego *I* to awareness of the larger consciousness that is the very fabric of the universe. You will come to see that your individual awareness is never truly separate from this greater consciousness; you merely experience it as separate while you have a body, a physical form. Like a wave in the sea, you are a distinct and unique individual, but at the same time you are never separate from the sea itself, from your source. Embodiment in itself is a temporary state. Your body is your local self, while the vast sea of infinite consciousness is your nonlocal self. Once you receive One Spirit Medicine and recognize your nonlocal, infinite nature, you can return to your everyday, local, embodied awareness knowing that you have the power to envision a new reality—even to grow a new body that ages and heals differently.

The journey to the East is an inner journey to the heavenly realms beyond death, where you are shown the vastness of creation. But the visionary has a duty to bring this knowledge back home. While many mystics seek to reach the farthest heavenly realms and stay there in blissful contemplation, the shaman is intent on creating heaven on earth, on returning to ordinary reality to help others taste the delicious elixir of One Spirit. Like the shamans, we practice healing and generosity and bring beauty to the world without any thought to what's in it for us. In fact, for the shaman the opportunity to alleviate suffering is reward enough.

As it happens, there *is* a reward for the visionary, however. You will discover that you can create extraordinary health for yourself. This doesn't mean you have to instruct individual genes to switch on or off, or tell your brain which neurotransmitters to produce. You simply hold the dual eagle vision of your life—both the details and the immensity of creation—and your body will do the rest. Just as stress switches on the genes that create cardiovascular disease and cancer, the serenity that eagle vision brings switches on the genes for health and longevity. As eagle vision dissolves the illusion of separation, you create the conditions for health, and disease can vanish.

When you go on your vision quest—whether following the template laid out in Chapter 13 or some other form—you are invited to travel to a realm beyond death and retrieve your destiny from the "future you" who already exists in timelessness. Once you encounter who you will be many lifetimes from now, you can begin to embody those qualities and attributes today. The past that stalked you will give way to a future that draws you inexorably toward the self you're becoming, the self who needs no interventions or therapies or repairs. You won't have to heal what's broken—healing will take care of itself.

Some of the tribes in the Amazon have a different notion of time from ours. In my early travels with the Amazon shamans, they told me how they were able to journey to "a long time from now"—many years in the future—and then bring the vision and wisdom they discovered back to the present. This was somewhat like doing a soul retrieval, they said, only instead of journeying to the past to retrieve what had been lost, they were tracking destiny in the future.

At the time, this ability was incomprehensible to me, as I came from a culture where time was linear and flowed in only one direction. Later, I learned about the shamans' belief that in the journey of the visionary, you are able to step into timelessness, freed from the constraints of past and future in the ever-present now. Sometimes a shaman was able to find a healed state in the future for a patient, and then sit back and watch how destiny pulled the patient toward the desired state of health. This ability reduced the amount of *doing* the shaman had to engage in. Practicing non-doing, he fixed things in the non-ordinary world.

Rumi, in his poem "The Night Air," describes the non-doing of the person who has completed the journey of the East:

> Mystics are experts at laziness. They rely on it,
> Because they continuously see God working all around them.
> The harvest keeps coming in, yet they
> Never even did the plowing![1]

But before we can reach the point of non-doing, there is work to be done. The path of the eagle is not for someone looking for a quick route to a happy life. For nearly all of us, the approach to One Spirit Medicine is a long and winding road. The story of Siddhartha, the Indian prince who became the Buddha, illustrates the journey of the eagle: the awakening of vision, the call to destiny, and the return to the world to share what we've learned.

SIDDHARTHA: THE GIFTS OF ONE SPIRIT MEDICINE

According to legend, the Buddha was born a prince, Siddhartha—whose name means "all wishes fulfilled." His father was a great king who was determined to keep his son from experiencing the anxiety and pain of the world. He was the ultimate helicopter parent, sheltering young Siddhartha from all ugliness. The prince grew up surrounded by flowering gardens and attended by servants who catered to his every need, oblivious to what was happening outside the palace walls where the commoners lived. Like Siddhartha, we want to live in a bubble of happiness and comfort, forever removed from anything that might cause us distress. His father represents our tendency to isolate ourselves, to build our own little palace in the middle of the slums and focus on our own needs, oblivious to the discomfort of others.

But human beings are social animals, attuned to one another's cues, empathizing with one another's pain, and wired to experience sadness at the sight of someone else's suffering. One day, after Siddhartha had left childhood behind, he became curious about what went on outside the palace. Against his father's wishes, he asked his charioteer to drive him around the countryside so he could see the people he would rule one day and understand how they lived. For Siddhartha to mature, he had to break out of the psychic bubble of his childhood.

As he rode in his regal chariot, Siddhartha came upon four sights that unsettled him deeply. The first was an old man, hobbling along on the side of the road, groaning in pain. "Why is he groaning?" Siddhartha asked his driver. The driver replied, "Because he is old and infirm, so he suffers."

This was a huge wake-up call for Siddhartha, who had never imagined such things as aging and infirmity. He had heard of suffering but didn't believe it existed, yet here it was right in front of him. "Will I grow old and become infirm?" he asked. "Yes," his driver said.

Wealthy, well fed, and groomed to rule the entire kingdom from his cocoon of luxury, Siddhartha wasn't in any pain, but his response to seeing someone else suffer was to ask, *What about me?* Later, after he became a Buddha, he turned this worry into compassion for others, no longer focusing on his own vulnerability. We are all responsible for our own well-being, but that's very different from "looking out for number one" and putting our needs ahead of everyone else's.

It's no accident that the first suffering Siddhartha encountered was a man who was soon to leave behind his old life and experience death. Siddhartha was leaving behind his old life of comfort and entering into an unfamiliar realm of uncertainty: *How long will I live? How long can I avoid infirmity? Who am I, if not a prince so powerful that I will live forever, happy all the time?* It pained him to discover there was nothing he could do to restore the old man's youth and vitality. *So much for being the all-powerful ruler of the land,* Siddhartha thought. He had to discard that role, he realized.

The first sight on the road corresponds to the First Noble Truth of Buddhism: in life, there is suffering. This is the truth we come to accept when we do the work of the South on the medicine wheel, shedding outmoded roles and victim identities to give birth to a nobler role as the author of our own destiny.

Siddhartha was still wondering if death was a long way off when he saw another sight that distressed him: a naked, diseased man by the side of the road, begging for coins or food. "Driver," Siddhartha asked, "what's wrong with that man?"

Siddhartha's driver replied, "That's a hungry, naked, diseased beggar." And then Siddhartha asked, "Might I be like that beggar someday?" "Yes," said the driver, "because even though you're rich and will rule over the entire land, you won't have the power to avoid disease. You, too, will grow old, and lose your health and beauty."

Siddhartha was shocked. He had no idea there would ever be an end to his robust good health or his ability to realize his desires, but now he was hearing that such an outcome was inevitable. *There must be a mistake,* he thought. *This might happen to others, but could it really happen to me?* We all want to believe we are safe, that bad things only happen to other people. When we are young we learn that people grow old and die, but we never believe that will happen to us.

Siddhartha's revelation at the sight of the beggar corresponds to the Second Noble Truth: Suffering is caused by attachment. Our happiness depends on having what we want and not having what we don't want. When we're content, we don't want anything to change. Instead of realizing that change is inevitable, and looking forward to what else might come along and delight us, we cling to the old, until our closets are filled with old clothing, our cellars with old stuff, and our minds with old thoughts and beliefs. Sometimes we even become attached to a bad situation—an abusive marriage or a terrible job—thinking, *It's probably better than being single at 50 or not having any work.* Afraid of uncertainty, we cling to old roles and identities, even though they no longer fit. But the way forward is to let go of our old roles and attachments— to release them into the fire, as we did in the journey of the healer. We have to die to our old notions and let our expectations change as we go forth into the unknown.

When I received my diagnosis of "you should be dead," my long list of what I needed to be happy was suddenly wiped clean. The only things that mattered were my health and, if that couldn't be restored, preparing to die. Today, I purposely keep my happiness list very short, with those two items at the very top.

We're attached not only to what's in the past—what we've outgrown but still keep in our closets—but also to what the future may bring. We cling to the idea that life will get better. The notion that something unpleasant might await makes us freeze in fear. The diseased man whom Siddhartha encounters represents our primal survival fears: not having enough food, money, health, or power. The old man is the future we dread and attempt to avoid at all costs. But when we face our fear of death in the journey of the jaguar and learn to walk through the jungle of uncertainty, we cease to cower helplessly in terror at the unknown.

Siddhartha, however, was still unnerved by the possibility of his own sickness and decline when he came across a third distressing sight alongside the road: a corpse.

"What's wrong with him? Why isn't he getting up and going about his business?" Siddhartha asked his driver. "He's dead," said the driver.

"There's no way to bring him back to life?" Siddhartha asked. "Alas, no," came the answer.

Siddhartha was deeply saddened. "Will my life also end someday?" Indeed, the driver told him, death is inevitable for all.

The corpse alongside the road corresponds to the Third Noble Truth: To end suffering, we have to release all attachments, even the attachment to life itself. We have to stop grasping at what is slipping away from us, or yearning for what we've lost and can't seem to regain. And we have to stop believing that inner peace comes only when our wishes come true.

Upon hearing that he, too, would someday die, Siddhartha was very upset. But there was one last sight that would shake his awareness: a sadhu, or holy man, sitting cross-legged in meditation beside the road. The man seemed utterly tranquil, beyond all fear and suffering. Siddhartha asked his driver to stop the carriage, and he hurriedly approached the sadhu to ask how he had achieved such serenity.

"You, too, can transcend suffering and death," promised the sadhu. "You need only sit still under that tree over there, refusing all food and drink, until you know that you are free from the death that is stalking you."

Siddhartha returned to the palace but found that life as he knew it had lost its appeal. The sadhu's words never left him. A few years later, he abandoned his life of riches and ease, and, drawn toward his destiny, set out as a wandering monk to find an end to his suffering. Once the veil is lifted and, like Siddhartha, we have a glimpse of suffering—the world's and our own—our old ways begin to chafe, and the quest for healing begins. How long or how fraught with challenges the journey of the visionary will be varies with the individual. But by now you have a pretty good idea that the road is steep and seldom straight, and that healing involves dedicated physical, mental, and emotional preparation.

Siddhartha spent six years in deep meditation, with little sustenance for his body, but still he was unable to find the answers he sought. Finally, in an act of desperation and surrender, he sat down under a fig tree and vowed not to move until he had discovered the cause of suffering and how to put an end to it. Children played around him, dogs barked, beautiful women tried to seduce or distract him, robbers took his monk's bag with his few possessions. But Siddhartha simply sat there, turning his gaze within, studying the nature of his own mind. He opened his heart and released any expectations about what would happen. And then, according to legend, after a harrowing night, at daybreak he experienced enlightenment under what was thereafter known as the Bodhi tree. (*Bodhi* means "awakened.") Later the Buddha described what he had awakened to:

> I came to direct knowledge of aging and death, direct knowledge of the origination of aging and death, direct knowledge of the cessation of aging and death, direct knowledge of the path leading to the cessation of aging and death . . .[2]

Whether we call it enlightenment, realization, awakening, or One Spirit Medicine, the experience that transformed Siddhartha into the Buddha, the Awakened One, was profoundly healing and, at the same time, disarmingly simple. "The truth of cessation is a personal discovery," the Tibetan Buddhist teacher Chögyam Trungpa Rinpoche said. "It is not mystical and it does not have any connotations of religion or psychology, it is simply your experience . . . It is like experiencing instantaneous good health: you have no cold, no flu, no aches, and no pains in your body. You feel perfectly well, absolutely refreshed and wakeful! Such an experience is possible."[3]

Siddhartha had set out to heal his own suffering, and from his quest he brought back to humanity the means to end their suffering in the face of disease, old age, and death. This is the gift of the eagle, the fruit of the journey of the visionary.

ONE SPIRIT MEDICINE REVEALED

In the direction of the East on the medicine wheel, you lose yourself to find yourself. Having died to the old, you are reborn into a new life. You realize that the local you who dwells in the physical world is ever changing, but the timeless, nonlocal you never changes and never suffers. The nonlocal you was never ill and will never die. This realization can help you return to perfect health.

We began our discovery of the timeless self in the South, where we shed our old roles and preconceived notions about who we really are and, like Parsifal, healed the wounded masculine within us. We continued the journey in the West, with Psyche teaching us that we had to cross a threshold into the unknown if we were going to free ourselves from the prison of our own fear, most notably our fear of death, and retrieve the gifts of the goddess, of immortality. Having accomplished that, in the North we learned to be still and focus inward, drawing on the collective wisdom of those who have gone before us. The splendor of the cosmos was revealed to us, just as it was to Arjuna.

When we reached the East, all the steps on the path, all the trials we endured, suddenly made sense. Opening to a wider perspective, we grasped the paradox of our existence: that each of us is both infinitesimal, a mere speck, and infinitely vast, simultaneously nothing and everything. Even enlightenment, we discovered, has a nothing-special, everyday side to it. And we learned that like Siddhartha, once we receive One Spirit Medicine, we must bring that healing to the world.

After his enlightenment, the Buddha taught the Four Noble Truths he had discovered under the Bodhi tree: there is suffering in life; suffering arises from attachment and desire; there is a way out of suffering; that way is the Eightfold Path, with skillful practices that support an awakened life. The essence of these timeless teachings is what we discover for ourselves when we receive One Spirit Medicine.

So, while you may intellectually grasp the lessons associated with the four directions on the medicine wheel, it is only with the direct experience of One Spirit that these principles take hold and shift your life. In the East, we have to confront our inner demons much as the Buddha—and Jesus—did. Jesus did not wrestle his demons to the ground; he simply told them firmly to be on their way. The Buddha, rather than fight his demons, fed them: "Here, you want my head, take it. You want my body, take it." His nonlocal self understood that he was not his body or his head, and when he failed to engage with his tormentors, they became bored and left. The great temptation for us is to battle our demons, thinking we can emerge victorious. And then 30 years later, scratched and bloodied, we finally recognize the futility of battle. One Spirit Medicine gives us a better way to move our demons along.

There's work to do after taking One Spirit Medicine, of course. Even when we've received the gifts of One Spirit, we still have to meet the challenges of our physical existence. And awakening doesn't absolve us of the need to refine our thinking and continually improve our attitudes and behavior. Even the Dalai Lama feels anger, he admits; despite his godlike qualities, he's only human. But he doesn't feed this anger or act upon it, so it quickly passes.

He approaches life with compassion and eagle vision: "I always look at any event from a wider angle," His Holiness told a *Time* magazine interviewer.[4] Jesus came back from the desert with the wisdom teachings of *Love your neighbor as yourself* and *Turn the other cheek*, but he did a lot of walking, teaching, and suffering before his work was done. The Buddha, after his enlightenment, didn't retreat to a mountaintop to dwell in bliss. For the next 45 years, he was very much in the world, helping others awaken and heal.

So how will *your* life be different after taking One Spirit Medicine? For one thing, the wider perspective of eagle vision will help you navigate your life with greater ease and compassion. The work you do will seem natural and effortless, consonant with your talents and desires. And the healing of body, mind, and spirit you experience will have such force behind it that you will feel compelled to serve the world however you can.

With that foretaste of what the journey of the visionary will bring, we can take the last step in the journey of the visionary: the vision quest. The guiding practice of the East, this is an age-old way to experience the transforming power of One Spirit.

CHAPTER 13

THE VISION QUEST

How do you apply quantum mechanics to everyday life? . . .
Does quantum theory teach you how to walk on the Earth?
How to change the weather? How to identify yourself with the
creative principle, with Nature, with the Divine? Does it teach
you how to live every moment of your life as an act of power?

It's one thing to read about One Spirit Medicine, and another to experience it. Just as reading about Siddhartha's enlightenment is not enough to free you from disease, old age, and death, reading about One Spirit Medicine will give you information but not wisdom. For that you must receive One Spirit Medicine directly. The final and most important practice for attaining it is the vision quest.

The vision quest can heal your body and mend your soul. Like Parsifal, you may search for the Holy Grail. Like Psyche, you may return from the underworld with the elixir of immortality. And like Arjuna, you may discover the secrets of the cosmos. But like Siddhartha, you must leave the comfort of the castle or the couch and sit under your version of the Bodhi tree.

We all have a dozen reasons for why we can't leave the castle or the couch just yet: not enough money, not enough time, too many e-mails to respond to. I myself postponed the final journey until I received a fateful diagnosis and saw the end of my life before me. My advice? Don't wait until then!

Ideally, you will make your vision quest in a natural setting, as the shamans do, sitting with the elements—rain, wind, sun, heat, cold—and putting your body under mild physiological stress by fasting. However, the purpose of a vision quest is not to rough it without food or water but to discover in the wilderness that you are a citizen of the earth, a child of nature, at one with all creation. You fast to awaken the body's self-repair systems and stimulate production of stem cells in the brain and every organ in your body.

Unless you upgrade your brain first, however, the vision quest will be nothing more than a camping trip. But when you detox and then power your brain with superfoods, the quest can be a face-to-face meeting with your destiny in which you discover your ability to co-create with Spirit. If you have applied yourself diligently to the practices suggested throughout the book, you will almost certainly taste the Oneness of creation as you receive One Spirit Medicine.

TAKING THE CHALLENGE

"What do you mean, a vision quest?" Sally, an inveterate New Yorker, demanded. "You know I don't rough it, and this means I don't go anywhere without room service!" A city girl inside and out, Sally was a high-powered editor at a women's fashion magazine. She wanted no part of being in the wilderness alone for three days, subsisting on nothing but water.

"But do you want to be miserable for the rest of your life?" I asked her. "Wouldn't it be better to be miserable for three days and get it over with, so you can have a new life? Besides," I added slyly, "there's probably a good magazine article in there as well."

Reluctantly, Sally agreed to do a vision quest, and I dropped her off, kicking and screaming, in a box canyon—a canyon surrounded by steep cliffs—in the red rocks of southern Utah. She had plenty of water and a good tent and a sleeping bag. I did not explain to her that although nature is the preferred setting for a vision quest, in fact you could do one anywhere, even in the middle of New York City. The point is to disconnect from the technologically wired world and discard the belief that if you aren't continually checking your e-mail and social media, your life will fall apart. I also instructed Sally to pray.

"But I don't know how to pray," she protested.

"Give thanks to the Creator," I told her. "And if that doesn't work," I said offhandedly as I drove off, "pray that the wolves won't get you." There were no wolves in the area, but Sally got my point. We can find our way to Spirit through prayer or meditation, but if we get caught up in exactly *how* we're supposed to pray or communicate with Spirit, we'll remain closed to the messages we might receive.

Sally was a longtime client. Rich and smart, she had been a beauty in her 20s, and even in her mid-50s was undeniably glamorous. She was also hyperkinetic, used to getting her own way, and cursed with the worst luck in relationships of anyone I've ever met. Sally was taking Ritalin during the day to manage her ADHD, and trazodone, a powerful antidepressant and antianxiety drug, to help her sleep at night. She kept bouncing from one abusive relationship to the next, to the point where she had become so desensitized that she preferred, as she put it, "to use men as toys." But she also admitted she could not get rid of those toys without a lot of heartache.

The vision quest challenged many of Sally's city comfort habits. There was no gourmet grocery store nearby. She could not switch on the news, and there was no Internet. She hated the thought of being in the wild by herself. But she could not bear the idea of continuing her life of romantic wretchedness and pharmaceutical misery.

"I loved peeing in the woods," Sally told me with a grin when I picked her up at the end of the three days. Her hair was disheveled and her face full of grime, but somehow her clothing was impeccable. I wondered how she had managed that. Then she admitted she had brought a clean outfit for each day. (Some habits die hard.) The retreat had not been easy for her, she said. On day one she tried calling a car service to come and get her, but there was no cell phone connection. At night, she was convinced she would be food for the wolves and imagined them circling her tent. She prayed for dawn to arrive. But by the second evening, she began to enjoy watching the stars from inside her sleeping bag, which she dragged out of the tent when she realized she wasn't going to attract a pack of hungry predators. Sally had never seen so many stars in the sky—in fact, had not seen stars at all for years, since the city lights of New York make it hard to see anything in the night sky. Hunger pangs kept her awake the first evening, but after that she slept like a baby. And then there were the lights. "During the first night I felt like I was camping in a parking lot," she said. "There were headlights shining into the tent, so bright that they woke me up. But when I went outside, it was perfectly dark, except for the stars." At first Sally thought extraterrestrials had been shining the lights, but then she realized that in her dreams she was being shown "the light."

Sally came back from her vision quest with a deep appreciation for nature and for how precious her life—indeed, all life—is. She continued eating the superfoods in the program, and I performed several Illuminations to clear imprints in her luminous energy field. At one point we had to release the soul of her mother, who had been dead for 13 years but had attached herself to Sally's luminous energy field.

Sally also decided to take a hiatus from men. She began to see her immediate attraction to certain men as a warning sign that they weren't the kind who would be good to her. Then six months after her vision quest, she started dating a quiet, gentle man—a "really soft man," in her words. But the most notable change after her vision quest was that Sally's ADHD mysteriously went away. As she remained on a gluten-free, dairy-free diet incorporating healthy foods like quinoa, her hyperactivity and moodiness dissipated, and she no longer required Ritalin to function during the day or trazodone to sleep at night.

THE BREAD MAKER

When Samuel came to see me, he weighed 260 pounds. He ate almost nothing but bread, pasta, and processed foods, and he had high blood pressure, elevated cholesterol, and insulin resistance. Samuel was a publisher whose list included books on health, raw foods, and healthy diets, yet he was a compulsive eater. Addicted to processed carbs, which turn into sugar almost as soon as you eat them, Samuel was suffering from *diabesity*—diabetes associated with obesity. It's the new epidemic of the civilized world. I mentioned to Sam that incidences of type 1 diabetes, in which the pancreas is unable to produce any insulin, had dropped 60 percent during World War II as a result of food scarcity. I told him that fasting during his vision quest would give him the same benefit, without starving him for more than a few days.[1]

Samuel had tried every diet plan in the world and at that point was following the Paleo diet. As I described in Chapter 5, the Paleo diet is based on what preagricultural, Paleolithic-era humans ate. Hunter-gatherers, they subsisted mostly on greens and the occasional small game or fish they could scavenge by simple hunting techniques. "Brilliant," I told him. "That's the One Spirit Medicine diet: lots of proteins and healthy fats, and no processed carbs." There are no essential carbs, I explained to him, but there are essential proteins and fatty acids, and we could live the rest of our lives without ever eating another piece of toast. "It's the processed carbs that make you fat, not the fats," I emphasized. I suggested that Samuel also stay away from red meat—beef and pork.

"But red meat is part of the Paleo diet," he protested.

I have lived in the Amazon with people who eat the same way their ancestors have eaten for millennia, and while they eat a lot of fish, they seldom consume red meat. We evolved with the plants, I explained. And hunter-gatherers didn't have weapons that could bring down large animals. "It's fine to have an occasional piece of red meat," I told Samuel. "But when you do, be sure it's grass fed and free-range, not from animals that were grain fed or pumped full of antibiotics. Fish, if they come from clean water and contain no mercury, are great. But the bread and pasta have to go."

While many people embrace the Paleo diet, they forget to embrace the Paleolithic beliefs about the Oneness of all life, the communion with nature and Spirit. "Those beliefs are a big part of creating health in your body," I told Samuel. "The diet alone doesn't work without Spirit being enlisted to help you change your ways."

Samuel was a tough cookie. He assured me he would put away his bread-making machine, but his cupboards were filled with canned foods, most of which contained wheat products and therefore gluten. Samuel wasn't going to give up gluten easily.

So one afternoon we went to his apartment, and I started emptying his cupboards, tossing out canned foods, wheat flour that was stored in the closet next to the bread-making machine, and the bread-making machine itself. He even had toothpaste that contained gluten! As I was taking it all out to the garbage chute, I could tell that Samuel was distraught. He loved his bread machine, and deep in his mind he believed he simply had to put it away for a brief hiatus. But here I was throwing away his beloved contraption!

When we're young, our mothers give us food to comfort us, so from then on when we feel stressed we tend to gravitate to comfort foods—the sugary treats we grew up on. The result is that over the decades, the marvelous flora in our guts become addicted to sugars, carbs, and nasty fats, so when we fast for more than 12 hours, the digestive flora go into revolt. *We're* not starving, but *they* are, so they begin releasing chemical toxins that signal starvation to the brain. Even though we don't actually need nourishment, we become ravenously hungry, simply because the flora want to feed.

The gut microbes are extraordinarily smart, however, and they learn very quickly. In just 24 hours, we can break their food addictions and begin to establish a new balance in the colony, allowing good flora to flourish. Cutting off sugars, starches, and harmful fats and taking quality probiotics allow the good bugs to recolonize your gut. That's why very short bouts of fasting are so important: they restore the balance in the gut and turn on all the body's repair systems.

Samuel knew intellectually that processed carbs like bread and pasta are extremely addictive, stimulating the same reward centers in the brain that cocaine does. He had badly damaged his gut with all the gluten and processed food he had been consuming for years, but that wasn't enough to convince him to make the changes necessary to heal his body and reclaim his life. That day by the garbage chute, we almost had a fistfight. It was the first time since high school that someone had shoved me against a wall!

Not everyone has to treat gluten as a toxin, but it was clear that Samuel wasn't going to break his habit and begin to repair his brain unless he went cold turkey. Finally, grudgingly, he agreed to the changes I was imposing, but only because he had run out of excuses.

What happened next was miraculous. Within four days, Samuel began to feel better and lose weight—more than a pound a day. And he was doing it by eliminating gluten, wheat, carbs, dairy, coffee, and sugars from his diet, and taking the detoxifying supplements I recommended in Chapter 4. It wasn't easy. A couple of times he called me during the night crying, as images from his unhappy childhood and adolescence kept flooding his mind. By the end of week two, however, Samuel had lost close to 20 pounds, and his brain fog had cleared. He was sleeping soundly for the first time in decades. And the detoxifying supplements were helping him eliminate the toxins previously stored in his fat, so that they would not be reabsorbed by his gut. Samuel was ready for the vision quest.

While God seems to prefer churches, Spirit seems to prefer wild places. In fact, nearly all the memorable encounters with the divine recorded in myth and history have occurred in a natural setting—the wilderness, a mountaintop, the desert—but seldom inside a cathedral. Samuel decided he would do his vision quest at the Fairchild Tropical Botanic Garden in Coral Gables, Florida, near his summer home. He would go to the Gardens at seven every morning when the park opened and remain on the grounds until it closed. His task was to speak to no one and simply to sit in the shade of the trees he enjoyed most and drink lots of water throughout the day.

After his three-day vision quest, Samuel told me, "While I didn't meet God, I discovered a quiet that I had known only as a child. After the second day, my mind stopped thinking about all the important things I had to do. I'd always felt that if I didn't do all those things, the world would end. The tropical trees showed me that I was like them—shedding leaves, budding with new growth, needing deep roots to hold me up during the high winds and storms—and that it was my job to help create a world that was not ruined by human folly and greed.

"The most difficult part was the grumbling in my stomach," he said. "For the first time in my life, I experienced real hunger. At first, all I could think about was a chocolate bar I had in my car. But after day two, my obsession with feeling hungry passed. After day three, I think I could have gone without food for another week. The physical discomfort of not eating was gone, and I felt tremendous energy. My head was clear and lucid, and I felt a tremendous sense of peace."

I continued working with Samuel for another year, and he remained free of wheat and dairy. We did Illuminations every two weeks to clear the imprints of anger, obesity, and heart disease from his LEF. He had rescued his bread machine from the garbage chute, but he never brought it out again, and after six months, his blood-sugar levels returned to normal. We did regular blood tests of IGF-1, a tumor marker, and found that his levels decreased by more than 30 percent.

Today, Samuel is a practicing Zen Buddhist. "It's the most non-religious religion I could find," he explained. During his vision quest, he discovered an inner life he had read about in the books he published but had never been entirely convinced was real. Because of his meditation practice, he now explores his inner world with the same sense of adventure that early explorers must have felt as they discovered new lands in the Americas. He is fascinated by the joyous landscapes of his mind, which he is finally able to access, instead of ruminating on his To Do list and regrets about his childhood.

RETURNING TO LIFE

George, a physician, was literally dragged into my office by his wife. He was going through a very aggressive chemotherapy that was not producing the desired results. His tumor markers were not budging, and his immune system was suppressed. He had agreed to see me only because his wife, a student at our Light Body School, had pointed out that he had nothing left to lose.

George did not see the relationship between his stressful job, his caffeine intake—half a dozen cups of coffee a day—his carb-heavy diet, and his cancer.

My friend, doctor Dean Ornish, in his clinical research at the University of California Medical Center, discovered that patients with prostate cancer who switched to a primarily plant-based, low-calorie diet could dramatically reverse early-stage cancers within a six-month period.[2] It's amazing the power that green plants have to switch on the genes that create health and switch off the genes that create disease. I immediately asked George to go on a plant-based diet rich in cruciferous vegetables, including broccoli and Brussels sprouts, and healthy fats like avocados and walnuts. He was to begin each morning with a detoxifying green juice. I asked him to steer clear of gluten and all grains, and to avoid red meat.

After decades of eating the toxic fast-food fare in the hospital, in just three weeks George lost nearly ten pounds. He was feeling better every day, and the tumor markers were beginning to recede.

"Now we have to do your vision quest," I told him. The last time George had been out in nature, he said, was as a Boy Scout 40 years earlier. When he wasn't working in the hospital, he spent all his quality time with his children, so he didn't feel he should take a weekend to go into the wild alone.

"I'll do my vision quest in the hospital, while I'm working," he decided. "I might be a little fog-brained at first, but that's not a problem. When an emergency case comes through, the adrenaline allows me to shake off any mental fog right away."

George's hospital was a trauma center in Miami, and I asked him to say a prayer for each patient he treated. And I suggested that while he was patching them up, he should admire the beauty of the blood vessels, muscles, and other tissues that make up the body. I also told him to be mindful of seeing each of his patients as a human being, not as a gunshot wound or diagnosis. Of all the things I asked him to do, he said this was the hardest, because like most doctors, he had been trained to view patients impersonally, maintaining professional distance. Most doctors, afraid perhaps of being overwhelmed by their feelings in the face of great suffering, are more comfortable relating to symptoms and organs than to living, breathing, terrified patients.

"Understand that you are doing Spirit's work every time you touch someone," I told him, "and bless each one of your patients with a prayer or a thought."

Whatever your profession, once you understand that Spirit's work can become *your* work—that Spirit can work through your hands, your heart, your feelings, your skills—your life acquires greater meaning. George told me that the wildest time in the ER seems to be during a full moon, when the number of patients coming in with gunshot wounds, injuries from accidents, or drug and alcohol overdoses appears to be greater than at any other time of the month. George began his vision quest during a full moon and decided he would practice monitoring his breath to remain mindful of what he was experiencing and to connect with each patient as a human being rather than as "the gunshot wound in Bed 6." He tried to note each inhalation and exhalation, and in the moment of stillness between breaths, he would pause, appreciating every precious drop of air. As he was breathing, he repeated to himself, *I am inhaling health, vitality, love, and forgiveness with every breath.*

"I can do without the food," George told me, "but I know that I can't do without the coffee." I enjoy coffee myself, and I could understand George's predicament. In fact, coffee is used as a sacred medicine in many parts of the world. The Sufi whirling dervishes are notorious coffee drinkers. And coffee, perhaps more than any other food, is a powerful activator of cellular detox pathways and the longevity proteins in the body. No one knows exactly how or why this works, but even oncologists today are recommending that liver cancer patients drink three to four cups of the black stuff each day. But if you're stressed out and living in a constant state of fight-or-flight, caffeine only exacerbates the problem. I explained to George that it was essential that he stop drinking coffee at least a week before his vision quest began. He needed to give his frayed nervous system a much-needed rest.

When I saw George at my office two weeks after his week-long vision quest, he was exhilarated. He had given up coffee, cheating only twice with an espresso at the start of the week. The first day of fasting, he felt incredibly weak and hungry. But he concentrated on seeing every patient, no matter how dirty or broken, as an angel in the making. He found himself touching people he would never before have come near except with latex gloves and an air of detachment: a homeless man drenched in his own urine, a thug with a bullet in his leg. By day three, George had tapped into an extraordinary reservoir of energy. His hunger pangs had dissipated, he was drinking a lot of water, and he was amazed at how much he was defecating every day, given that he was eating no food whatsoever. His body was cleansing and detoxing, eliminating decades of waste that had built up in his digestive tract.

By day three, George had switched over to the ketone system, burning fats instead of sugars to fuel his body and brain. As his higher brain switched on, he was able to envision a life of health and well-being for himself. And from his newfound vantage point, he redefined his work. He was no longer a mechanic fixing arms and stomachs and broken bones; he was an artist helping people return to health from the brink of death. Last time I spoke with George, his cancer was in remission. He has recovered his life.

COMMUNION WITH CREATION

One Spirit Medicine allows you to experience communion with Spirit and understand the workings of creation. This understanding is not academic or intellectual; it's kinesthetic and sensory—a *knowingness* that pervades every cell of your body. You don't suddenly have a eureka moment and comprehend the first law of thermodynamics and the conservation of energy. Instead, you experience a transcendent awareness that penetrates your whole being. You truly grasp that energy and consciousness can never be destroyed, only transformed into myriad shapes and forms, one of which happens to be you.

Each of my clients mentioned in this chapter—Sally, Samuel, and George—experienced a deep, intuitive understanding of the wonder and miracle of One Spirit Medicine. For Sally, this new consciousness arose as she lay in the desert under the night sky, watching the stars that she knew had always been there, hidden behind the light pollution of New York City. For Samuel, observing his hunger and cravings, and realizing how much he loved to grapple with profound issues led him to a deeper exploration of his mind. He began by defining a problem, any problem, and then asking himself, *Who is it who is thinking about this? Who is it who is asking the question?* Those questions eventually led him to Zen, a meditation practice stripped of all adornment, in which the practitioner simply observes his breath and witnesses the mind in all its madness and creativity. As for George, he learned that he could see Spirit in everyone and, indeed, *needed* to see Spirit in everyone in order to become a better doctor and healer. In the process, he healed himself.

Each of these individuals came back to see me several more times, even when there was nothing obviously wrong, nothing that had to be repaired. They wanted more of the One Spirit Medicine that had healed them physically and emotionally. I did preventive Illuminations with them, to help clear any residual imprints of disease from the luminous energy field.

Normally, healing the spirit is the last step for people seeking healing in our society, but often it's the first step for those seeking One Spirit Medicine. The vision quest that Sally, Samuel, and George each undertook was the same sort of retreat, the same sort of quest for Spirit, that Jesus and the Buddha undertook. They confronted the demons of hunger, anger, and self-judgment. Their vision quests repaired their bodies and primed their brains for their great missions. They returned home afterward with a newfound sense of purpose, and a mission to share what they'd learned with humanity.

During a second vision quest, Sally had a dream that answered a central question: *What is the theme for the next stage of my life?* I had previously explained to her that you can't solve problems in your dreams with your "sugar brain," but with her brain properly healed, she was able to access uncommon wisdom. Here's the dream as she related it to me:

> *I'm in the past, centuries ago, and I tell my beloved I'll find him again and not to worry. I go through a glass door—it is our time to say good-bye—and suddenly, I'm in a museum, in the present. I'm amazed by my modern clothing. A man is there with me. I realize I must look for my beloved here and wonder, Is it this man? He turns and tells me that he is not the one I am looking for, but he will take me to the one I am seeking. I am*

searching for the Beloved—not the human beloved, but Spirit.
And Spirit is already walking by my side.

"In the dream there was deep familiarity," Sally said, "as if my beloved had always been there. And I felt that in a previous life-time I had also been searching for God." She realized that she was not only looking for the right partner but also searching for Spirit, the only lover who would truly fulfill her. She understood that she had to find Spirit *in* her partner and together *with* her partner.

POWER ANIMALS

In shamanic cultures, when you do a vision quest, traditionally a power animal will appear to you in a dream or waking vision. The word *animal* comes from the same root as *anima*, Latin for soul, breath, the life force. Carl Jung used *anima* to refer to the feminine principle. An animal, then, is an expression of the feminine aspect of the soul of the world. The power animal symbolizes the wild, undomesticated aspect of your being, the aspect that has no boss, isn't wedded to a laundry list, and is free as the wind. The power animal represents your unfettered soul, the part of you that hasn't been beaten down by the modern world.

If you visit certain caves in France and Spain, you can see ancient paintings of bears, bison, wolves, and other animals depicted by Paleolithic artists. The grace, power, dignity, and beauty of these creatures comes through with great intensity. The painting of "The Sorcerer" in the Trois-Frères cave in Ariège, France, depicts a mythic figure, part human and part stag, that is thought to be a shaman. Creatures that are part human and part animal represent our kinship with all animals.

To the humans of the Paleolithic period, animals were sacred. Today in the West, only our pets are sacred, and we eat meat from animals raised in the most inhumane ways and butchered in slaughterhouses, before being shrink-wrapped and sent to grocery stores. Humanity has a collective memory of our association with animals, however, and we see this in Native American cultures, where kinship is based on clans named for their totems: wolf, bear, rattlesnake, and the like. But those of us living outside tribal cultures are for the most part disconnected from Mother Earth and her seasons and creatures, and have little to no relationship with power animals of any kind.

Most of us would be hard-pressed even to name our state or national animal. Every state has a symbolic animal, like California's grizzly bear and Colorado's bighorn sheep. Similarly, countries have symbolic animals. The rooster is associated with France, the bear with Russia, and the panda with China. The eagle is the national symbol of at least eight countries, including the United States.

When you connect with a power animal you are in effect connecting with the psyche or soul of nature. During your vision quest, you will invite a power animal to come to you and teach you its ways. You do this by simply stating your intention in the form of a prayer. For example: *Great Spirit, creator of all, bless me with a visit from one of your creatures that will bring me a wisdom and strength I need in my life at this time.*

When you first encounter a Spirit animal, you may have no idea why that particular creature has come to you. Just accept its presence and remember that the power animal is an emissary from Spirit, come to guide you in taking the next step in your development. Power animals are protectors and teachers.

Sally brought a wolf back from her vision quest—the very animal she was most afraid would make a meal of her. When I asked her what the wolf symbolized to her, she said she felt it had come to teach her about belonging to a pack. The wolf ranges far, traveling alone, but always returns home to its mate. And wolves mate for life, or at least practice serial monogamy, which is a lesson Sally very much wanted to learn, once she found the right partner.

On his vision quest, Samuel encountered a squirrel in a dream; it offered him an acorn and then snatched it back, scratching Samuel's face in the process. His dream befuddled both of us for a while, until I asked Samuel to hold a dialogue with this power animal. There are several ways to have a dialogue with a power animal, but in this case, I told Samuel to start by drawing a line down the center of a sheet of paper and writing his name on the left side, and then making a sketch of the power animal on the right side of the page.

In this method of dialoguing with a power animal, you start by asking the power animal, "Who are you?" Then you listen for a response and write down what the power animal says. Samuel's squirrel was clear that it had come to teach him not to hoard things. One of the first things the squirrel said was that it knew exactly how many acorns it needed to support it through the long winter and that more acorns would not mean more safety or security. Samuel understood that the acorns referred to his weight. He didn't need to store any more body fat for the long winter that would never come. And then he saw that his hoarding habit had been passed down to him through three generations of Jewish ancestors who had been persecuted, stripped of their possessions and property, and then forced to flee their countries. It was a defining moment for Samuel when he realized that he no longer needed to continue living the familial story of scarcity. The squirrel had come to teach him to spend more time scurrying through the trees and soaring as he jumped between branches, and less time storing food for the lean times.

When you retrieve a power animal during a vision quest, you are inviting into your life the qualities it represents. Through the animal, you can explore new facets of yourself. You can cultivate a relationship with a power animal by embodying it—by imagining that you are looking with the eyes of a jaguar, say, or bounding gracefully like a gazelle. Or you could do yoga or one of the martial arts that have postures or movements named for the animals they suggest. Think of yoga poses like camel, cobra, lion, and downward-facing dog, or tai chi moves with evocative names like Birds Returning to the Trees at Dusk, Dragon Sweeping Tail, and Heavenly Horse Flying Across the Sky, or the five styles of kung fu: tiger, leopard, crane, snake, and dragon.

Spend time dialoguing with your power animal whenever you can. Let it teach you how to walk softly on the earth and how to see things that are not obvious to human eyes. Your power awakens your animal instincts, which can serve you in all situations. These are not your primitive, predatory, me-first survival instincts but rather the ones that foster empathy for other species and allow you to live in balance and harmony with all nature.

A LIFE-CHANGING EXPERIENCE

A vision quest can change your life forever. It's impossible to forget the intense awakening to your luminous nature that comes as the hunger pangs subside. This awakening of higher perception—what some call enlightenment or a rebirth experience—lifts the veil between the visible and invisible worlds. With the veil lifted, you instantly become aware of your Oneness with Spirit and all creation.

The vision quest takes a commitment, and it will most likely cause you some physical and emotional discomfort. But it's a powerful way to begin your transformation, a means of jump-starting your personal evolution.

CREATING YOUR OWN THREE-DAY VISION QUEST

The solo vision quest is the final step in receiving One Spirit Medicine. Traditionally, it takes place in a natural setting. Fasting and meditation are the central practices to bring about a profound experience of awakening to Spirit and realizing your Oneness with all creation.

Before beginning a vision quest, be sure you have been following the 18-hour sugar fast described in Chapter 4 for at least three months. This will ensure that your body knows how to go into ketosis—the state of switching from glucose to fat as its energy source. Otherwise you will be hungry and miserable in the wilderness for three days without deriving the healing benefits of the vision quest.

The following suggestions will help make your three-day vision quest a success:

Location: To find a suitable location for the vision quest, imagine you are being led by a jaguar to a secluded spot in nature. Cats have an uncanny sense of where to lie, while dogs are always sniffing around, trying one spot and then another. Your imaginary cat will lead you true. Be sure the place is beautiful, safe, and sufficiently secluded so that you will not be interrupted by hikers.

If you choose not to go into the wilderness for your vision quest you can pick a place closer to home—even in an urban area. The stories of Samuel and George in this chapter offer ideas on choosing an alternative location.

Equipment: You can bring a sleeping bag and sleeping pad, and, if you wish, a tent. Be sure to pack a notebook or journal and a pen, so you can record your dreams and any memories or strong feelings that arise. Do *not* bring a computer or other electronic devices, or any reading material.

You can bring a cell phone but only to use in case of emergency. Be sure to inform a friend or family member (or if you're staying in a public park or preserve, a ranger) exactly where you're going to be. If you wish, you can ask someone to check on you once a day, preferably in the evening, as long as they don't distract you.

Setting the space: When you arrive at the spot for your vision quest, draw a circle about 20 feet in diameter around your tent. This is your spot, and you will stay inside this circle for the next three days, stepping out only to relieve yourself in the woods or behind a bush. (Pack a few plastic garbage bags for waste disposal.)

Fasting: Fasting is a central part of the vision quest. In addition to putting the body into ketosis, it detoxifies the cells during autophagy and turns on production of stem cells in the brain.

You will get hungry, and your stomach will start growling. Often, the growling will be louder in your head than in your stomach; your limbic brain misses glucose-rich food and believes it will die if it skips a meal. Turn the growling into an opportunity to observe how wild the mind is.

Along with hunger pangs, you will most likely experience mood swings, low energy, and irritability during the first day or so of fasting. Most of the discomfort comes from the fact that your body is detoxifying. During the first 24 hours of a fast, you will burn through all the glycogen stored in your liver, then you will begin burning protein from your muscles, including the heart. After that your body will go into ketosis and switch over to burning fats. You can tell when you've switched to burning fats because your hunger pangs will go away.

Fasting for three days is perfectly safe for most people in good health. If you have any concerns, check with your physician or health counselor before starting the vision quest. If you are diabetic, or taking medication, or dealing with acute illness, *do not* fast without first consulting a physician. There are many places where you can do a medically supervised fast, including our Center for Energy Medicine in Los Lobos, Chile, and Dr. Gabriel Cousens's Tree of Life Center in Patagonia, Arizona.

During your vision quest, listen to your body and follow its guidance. If at any time you feel very sick, or your blood sugar is dropping dangerously, break your fast. I always keep chocolate and some basic foods like nuts and dried fruit in my vehicle, in case of emergency. Knowing there's chocolate just a few yards away makes it harder to maintain your fast, but you can turn this longing into a meditation—another opportunity to observe the madness of the limbic mind.

Water: It's imperative to stay hydrated. You should drink at least four liters of water a day, so plan accordingly when you pack your provisions. If you are making your vision quest in an arid desert climate, you will need more water—closer to six liters a day. The rule is to pee every hour. If you're not peeing that often, you're not drinking enough water.

Boredom: You will be bored. Take boredom as an indication that you are getting close to the state of contemplation you want to be in. Boredom and restlessness are the result of the limbic brain thrashing about for attention. Stay with the boredom, knowing that this is part of the process. Like hunger, it will pass.

Time: Leave your watch at home. Checking the time will not make it go by any faster, and you are trying to step into timelessness. Set your inner clock by the sun and the stars.

Meditation: During the day, you can do the exercise "I Am My Breath" in Chapter 11. In the evening, if you light a fire or a candle, you can do the exercise on burning old roles and identities described in Chapter 9. (If you do light a fire or candle, be sure there is no brush nearby that could ignite. And be sure the fire is extinguished completely before you leave the area.)

Prayer: During your vision quest, pray, giving thanks for the beauty around you and for every breath you take. Give thanks for your hunger pangs or the wolves you are sure will devour you during the night. Practice praying with your heart and not with your head.

Ending your vision quest: Plan to end your three-day vision quest before nightfall on the third day. Before you leave the site, be sure to pick up all trash, and carry it out with you. Make sure you leave the place as you found it—or cleaner. Leave no trace.

CONCLUSION:

ONE SPIRIT MEDICINE AND BEYOND

*We shall not cease from exploration / And the
end of all our exploring / Will be to arrive where
we started / And know the place for the first time.*

—T. S. ELIOT

The future Buddha had to face many tests. As soon as he sat under the Bodhi tree he was approached by the demon-god Mara, the lord of death, with weapons in hand, surrounded by his army. Legend has it that all the protecting deities of the universe fled, terrified, yet Siddhartha remained unmoved. Even as the demon hurled thunderbolts and flaming arrows at him, they were transformed into flowers that landed at Siddhartha's feet. Finally the future Buddha reached down with his right hand to touch the ground, claiming his place, and the earth goddess herself appeared to bear witness to his illumination. With a mighty roar, she drove away the demon-god.

The lore says that in the long night leading to his enlightenment, the Buddha acquired three gifts: the divine eye of omniscient vision and knowledge of all his previous existences; understanding of karma and the chain of causality and release, or liberation; and the Four Noble Truths, the fundamental laws of existence. It is said that the Buddha considered keeping this wisdom to himself, doubting that humans were ready for such a teaching, but Brahma intervened, persuading him to share with men and gods the profound truths that he had discovered.

What do we do after receiving One Spirit Medicine? Do we, like the Buddha, go into the world and teach what we've learned? Do we long to escape the battlefield altogether, like Arjuna, distraught that we can't prevent the suffering of life? Or, "like most of the rest of us," as Joseph Campbell puts it, do we "invent a false, finally unjustified, image of oneself as an exceptional phenomenon in the world, not guilty as others are, but justified in one's inevitable sinning because one represents the good. Such self-righteousness leads to a misunderstanding, not only of oneself but of the nature of both man and the cosmos."[1]

The heroes and heroines—both mythic and real—whose journeys we have explored throughout these pages remind us that our goal is to establish a relationship with the universal guiding principle we call One Spirit. And then we can set about repairing the torn fabric of our own lives, our health, and humanity, which is sorely in need of any wisdom we can impart.

HEALING THE WORLD

So how, then, do we bring the healing gifts of One Spirit Medicine to the world? The global situation is increasingly disquieting on every level—political, economic, social, and environmental. The first decade of the 21st century was the hottest in recorded history. In 2007, climate experts told us that to avoid irreversible consequences, we would have to make sure the level of carbon dioxide in the atmosphere did not exceed 350 parts per million. But by 2014, we had already passed 400 ppm with no sign of slowing down. Biologists, directly linking the rate of animal and plant species extinction to greenhouse gas emissions, warn that we're on the brink of mass extinction. Mass extinctions have occurred only five times since life emerged on earth some 3.5 billion years ago. Now we're facing the sixth such catastrophic event.

When we're stuck in our old paradigms and beliefs, we assume that as individuals we're helpless to save the whales or the planet or humanity. It's true, none of us alone can halt terrorism, wipe out environmental toxins, stop the melting of the polar ice caps, or avert economic crisis. What we can do, however, is heal from the sicknesses that threaten our survival. We can heal our inner masculine, giving up war as a way to resolve conflict. We can heal our inner feminine, becoming stewards of the earth. And if we've learned nothing else from receiving One Spirit Medicine, it's that with Spirit and one another, we are continually co-creating the world. We can always do a better job.

One Spirit Medicine enhances the body's ability to eliminate toxins we're exposed to, whether they're pollutants in the air, or water, or our food, or the mental poisons of unhealthy thinking and belief systems. One Spirit Medicine also allows us to access our innate ability to upgrade the brain so that it supports the consciousness that creates health. And the bonus is that in helping ourselves, we also help the earth. As we discard toxic and predatory beliefs and behaviors we can participate in co-creating a sustainable way for everyone to live together on earth. If we fail at this, the human species could very well become the next dodo bird.

In the West, the quest for enlightenment is seen largely as an individual pursuit, a mystical adventure for one. Yet One Spirit Medicine is also social and political. As you heal your brain and bring your health span into line with your life span, you can take an enlightened perspective into your community, to protect the land, clean up the waterways, and broker peaceful interaction.

As the Lakota Sioux phrase *Mitakuye Oyasin*—"All my relations"—implies, we're all connected, all in this together. Recovery is reciprocal: heal yourself, heal the world; heal the world, heal yourself. Once you're dedicated to improving your own health and the health of earth and all her creatures, the Spirit world will rally behind you to support your commitment.

INNER HARMONY

Peace and harmony in the world begin with your inner world. Your gut is a world unto itself—an immensely complex ecosystem. And since your body is hosting ten times more microbial DNA than cells with your own DNA, learning to live harmoniously with the microbes inside you is clearly crucial to your survival. Sustainable health depends on learning to not just survive but thrive, in collaboration with all the bacteria, viruses, and other cells in your body.

Your body is your earth, the ground that your life rests on. Dumping noxious pharmaceuticals into it is shortsighted. We're now facing deadly bacterial outbreaks because of our overuse of antibiotics and antimicrobial cleansers, which has allowed ever-resourceful microbes to mutate into drug-resistant strains. Your health and the health of the planet rest on forging a new relationship with all creatures, including the microbes in your body and the mitochondria in your cells. Once you've stopped battling disease and have found inner balance and peace, you can begin to share this lifesaving knowledge with others.

FROM STEWARDS TO DREAMERS

Historically, the Abrahamic religions—Christianity, Judaism, and Islam—have privileged man over nature. To this way of thinking, our earthly home is merely a way station to the bliss of eternal life. Taking care of the planet and all its creatures has been largely left to chance—not humanity's responsibility, at any rate. To scientists, however, the need to assume care of the earth is more pressing. Most agree that we're overtaxing the planet and that it's up to us to save it—to make the tough political and economic choices we've been deferring to future generations.

After years of living in shamanic cultures, I'm very aware of how much the indigenous worldview differs from the scientific paradigm of the West, as well as Western religious views. To the indigenous, the welfare of the planet comes first. That includes the well-being of all earth's inhabitants equally, nonhuman and human alike. Indigenous peoples believe we must take care of the planet not because earth is a temporary home granted to us by a distant God but because it's Mother Earth herself—our permanent home, into which we are reborn lifetime after lifetime.

As Krishna tells Arjuna:

> Even as a person casts off worn-out clothes and puts on others that are new, so the embodied Self casts off worn-out bodies and enters into others that are new. . . . Weapons cut It not; fire burns It not; water wets It not; the wind does not wither It. . . . This Self cannot be cut nor burnt nor wetted nor withered. . . . Eternal, all-pervading, unchanging, immovable, the Self is the same forever.[2]

The shamans teach us that earth is the heaven we earn after a long journey through the Spirit realms, and we must tend it as our Eden. Otherwise, the planet may decide it is unsustainable to continue supporting the greediest of her children. And because we the greediest have commandeered most of the resources for our own use, we've put the rest of nature—the innocent—in jeopardy. For the healing and survival of earth, we need a new dream now, before the damage we do to earth is too great to allow her to recover without losing her children.

I love medieval cathedrals and have spent many hours praying in churches like Notre Dame in Paris, admiring their magnificent stained glass windows. Yet I'm always struck by how little attention most religious centers pay to the surrounding ecosystem. Granted, many churches and temples have beautiful landscaping, but there's never any doubt that the divine isn't meant to be found in the grass and trees but inside the sanctuary on the altar. We need to take a more shamanic view of the divine as a numinous force that pervades all creation—animal, vegetable, and mineral.

While we've trampled on the earth, the footprint of the ancients was very gentle. Granted, that's partly because there were so few of them and their technology was so basic. Progress has taken its toll on the earth's resources. We've altered the earth biochemically, and because we're generating waste so fast, even our biodegradable refuse has no time to break down and recycle back into the earth's systems.

CHOOSING EVOLUTION

Despite all the devastation we've wrought, however, there are hopeful signs. All around the globe, people are creating new forms to replace the old ones that have crumbled beyond repair, whether in infrastructure, government, the economy, health care, or social welfare. Institutions are adapting in response to current needs, and so are our bodies and our brains.

Adaptation refers to short-term changes in individuals or groups to make them better suited to their environment. In times of stress and global crisis like the present, we may become ill—or we may become extraordinarily healthy, if we learn to adapt and thrive in rapidly changing conditions. Compared to adaptation, evolution—long-term genetic change to ensure survival of the species—moves at a glacial pace. But there's evidence now that our physiology is about to make an evolutionary leap. Over the past 20,000 years, the human brain has been steadily shrinking in size, losing some 10 percent of its volume,[3] a cluster of neurons about the size of a tennis ball. In evolutionary terms, this is a dramatic change, and a prelude to what's known as quantum speciation, the leap that can occur when a species is threatened with extinction.

We're at an evolutionary threshold. In the past, we ensured our survival by killing off competing species—or in the case of the Neanderthals, our distant relatives. And we've decimated or obliterated more than a few furry, finned, or feathered species. A new evolutionary leap might allow our species to survive, but we can't make the leap using the archaic methods of the tyrant-king brain.

Collectively, there may be a biological imperative stirring within us for our survival, but how much better it would be to assure our survival through less violent means—through conscious evolution, in other words. One Spirit Medicine gives us access to states of consciousness that are crucial for physical, emotional, and spiritual evolution in the face of environmental crises and the economic, political, and social changes we face.

A DIFFERENT BRAIN

The jungle is a noisy place, and so is the virtual world of the Internet and social media. Undoubtedly the future belongs to those who are adapted to the virtual world—who are at home in the virtual jungle and aware of which snapping twigs to listen to and which to ignore.

The generation coming of age now was raised in a totally wired world. They've used technology to communicate since they were old enough to tap out a message on a digital screen. Today, e-mail, cell phones, online forums, and social media are the dominant ways we engage with one another on everything that matters in our lives, from supporting efforts to reduce the causes of global poverty to making plans with our friends for Saturday night. Now, every generation needs to be able to move between the virtual world and the world of the senses as easily as the jaguar moves between the visible and invisible realms.

As I write this, one of the most popular online games is *Minecraft*. In this virtual world, gamers are dreamers and creators. They work together to gather virtual elements to feed, clothe, and shelter their virtual selves as they imagine and build new world systems. Like the invisible worlds that mystics travel between, *Minecraft* players inhabit virtual worlds separated by a thin veil. One of the worlds is Survival, where zombies may kill you and resources may be scarce. Creative, by contrast, is a world where no one dies, where there are predators but they don't attack you, and where resources are in abundance at all times. But gamers claim it's no fun to play in Creative only. It would be very boring, they say, to avoid the challenges in the realm of predators, where players have to band together to survive.

Many gamers seem to prefer the virtual world of *Minecraft*—even in Survival mode—to living in the ordinary world of the senses. Perhaps that's because they've found that life in the physical world can be exhausting and alienating, while in *Minecraft* they've tapped into the secret of how to actively dream reality into being.

The virtual world, particularly gaming, has its dark side. But cyberspace is also where we can experience community, creativity, and collaboration. These are perennial values consistent with a One Spirit perspective. Before long, we may be able to upload our consciousness into the cloud, minimizing our corporeal existence and inhabiting a world of our making—*Minecraft* on a global scale. But even then, Mother Earth will be humanity's home, and we are charged with being her stewards.

OUT OF CHAOS COMES CREATION

The shamans believe that long ago, in the invisible world, the blueprint of creation was drawn. Chaos was turned into order, into the cosmos, through the actions of Earthkeepers who were able to dream new worlds into being, in much the same way gamers are creating virtual worlds today. Our earth was dreamed into being with the perfect conditions to sustain life, with steady temperatures in the narrow band between the freezing and boiling points of water.

Just as life on earth began in a primordial soup, today we again find ourselves in a primordial soup of creative potential. One Spirit Medicine shows us the big picture, and from that perspective we can turn chaos into order and beauty. Healing is one form of order. When we bring greater order and harmony to the body, illness disappears, and we recover. We create the conditions for health, and disease goes away. The limbic brain is wired to resist uncertainty, but chaos is the very stimulus that can trigger quantum leaps in evolution. The old thinking says if it isn't broken, don't fix it. One Spirit awareness suggests that if it isn't broken, we need to break it, so that new forms that can't be extrapolated from the old can emerge.

The biggest breakthroughs in brain science today are neuroplasticity—the brain's ability to change and adapt, forming new neural connections in response to our experiences and environmental demands—and epigenetics, changes in the way genes are expressed. From Chapter 3, Dethroning the Tyrant King, you now know that you can rewire your brain for cooperation and joy instead of competition and fear. And from Chapter 5, Superfoods and Super Supplements, you know that you can use a phytonutrient-rich diet to rebalance the microorganisms in your gut, creating health and mental clarity, and affecting your gene expression. Within this lifetime, you can actually experience a new body—the "new suit of clothes" that the *Bhagavad Gita* speaks about. Neuroplasticity and epigenetics tell us we don't have to suffer the illnesses of our ancestors or perpetuate their beliefs. We can experience states of physical well-being and mental acuity that we never thought possible, and wisdom we never imagined. And we can find peace.

The quest for inner peace may be one of the most fundamental human longings. There's a famous story about a seeker who comes to the Ch'an Buddhist master Bodhidharma and begs the great teacher to pacify his soul. "Bring me your soul, and I will pacify it," Bodhidharma tells him. "That's the problem," the seeker says. "I have looked for years, but I cannot find it." With that, Bodhidharma declares, "Your wish is granted." The seeker understands and leaves in peace.

What the seeker realizes is that the soul, the fundamental truth of who we are, isn't something separate from the body, the body politic, or One Spirit. It isn't something "out there" that can be found. As Joseph Campbell explains it, "Those who know not only that the Everlasting lives in them, but that what they, and all things, really are *is* the Everlasting, dwell in the groves of the wish-fulfilling trees, drink the brew of immortality, and listen everywhere to the unheard music of eternal concord."[4]

That is the promise and bliss of One Spirit Medicine.

ENDNOTES

INTRODUCTION

1. Saint John of the Cross, *The Poems of St. John of the Cross* (Chicago: University of Chicago Press, 1979), 19.

2. Stephen Mitchell, *Bhagavad Gita: A New Translation* (New York: Three Rivers Press, 2002), 107.

3. "Risk Factors," Alzheimer's Association: http://www.alz.org/alzheimers_disease_causes_risk_factors.asp.

4. "FastStats: Obesity and Overweight," Centers for Disease Control and Prevention (updated May 14, 2014): http://www.cdc.gov/nchs/fastats/obesity-overweight.htm.

CHAPTER 3

1. Vincent J. Felitti, M.D., et al., "Relationship of Childhood Abuse and Household Dysfunction to Many of the Leading Causes of Death in Adults. The Adverse Childhood Experiences (ACE) Study," *American Journal of Preventive Medicine* 14, no. 4 (May 1998): 245–258.

CHAPTER 4

1. "The Medicare Prescription Drug Benefit Fact Sheet," Kaiser Family Foundation, September 19, 2014: http://www.kaiseredu.org/Issue-Modules/Prescription-Drug-Costs/Background-Brief.aspx.

2. Chia-Yu Chang, Der-Shin Ke, and Jen-Yin Chen, "Essential Fatty Acids and Human Brain," *Acta Neurologica Taiwanica* 18, no. 4 (December 2009): 231–241.

3. "Profiling Food Consumption in America," chap. 2 in *Agriculture Fact Book,* United States Department of Agriculture, 20: http://www.usda.gov/factbook/chapter2.pdf.

4. Owen Dyer, "Is Alzheimer's Really Just Type III Diabetes?" *National Review of Medicine* 2, no. 21 (December 15, 2005): http://www.nationalreviewofmedicine.com/issue/2005/12_15/2_advances_medicine01_21.html.

5. Henry C. Lin, M.D., "Small Intestinal Bacterial Overgrowth: A Framework for Understanding Irritable Bowel Syndrome," *The Journal of the American Medical Association* 292, no. 7 (August 18, 2004): 852–858.

6. Els van Nood et al., "Duodenal Infusion of Donor Feces for Recurrent Clostridium difficile," *The New England Journal of Medicine* 368, no. 5 (January 31, 2013): 407–415.

7. Jess Gomez, "New Research Finds Routine Periodic Fasting Is Good for Your Health, and Your Heart," Intermountain Healthcare, April 3, 2011: http://intermountainhealthcare.org/about/careers/working/news/pages/home.aspx?NewsID=713.

CHAPTER 5

1. Hervé Vaucheret and Yves Chupeau, "Ingested Plant miRNAs Regulate Gene Expression in Animals," *Cell Research* 22 (2012): 3–5.

2. Jo Robinson, "Breeding the Nutrition Out of Our Food," *The New York Times,* May 25, 2013: http://www.nytimes.com/2013/05/26/opinion/sunday/breeding-the-nutrition-out-of-our-food.html?smid=pl-share.

3. Britta Harbaum et al., "Identification of Flavonoids and Hydroxycinnamic Acids in Pak Choi Varieties (*Brassica campestris* L. ssp. *chinensis* var. *communis*) by HPLC-ESI-MSn and NMR and Their Quantification by HPLC-DAD," *Journal of Agricultural and Food Chemistry* 55, no. 20 (October 3, 2007): 8251–8260.

4. Haitao Luo et al., "Kaempferol Inhibits Angiogenesis and VEGF Expression Through Both HIF Dependent and Independent Pathways in Human Ovarian Cancer Cells," *Nutrition and Cancer* 61, no. 4 (2009): 554–563.

5. Sally Fallon and Mary G. Enig, Ph.D., "Lacto-fermentation," for the Weston A. Price Foundation, January 1, 2000: http://www.westonaprice.org/food-features/lacto-fermentation.

6. Martha Clare Morris, Sc.D., et al., "Consumption of Fish and N-3 Fatty Acids and Risk of Incident Alzheimer Disease," *Archives of Neurology* 60, no. 7 (July 2003): 940–946.

7. J. S. Buell, Ph.D., et al., "25-Hydroxyvitamin D, Dementia, and Cerebrovascular Pathology in Elders Receiving Home Services," *Neurology* 74, no. 1 (January 5, 2010): 18–26.

8. Michael F. Holick, M.D., Ph.D., "Vitamin D Deficiency," *The New England Journal of Medicine* 357, no. 3 (July 19, 2007): 266–281.

9. Parris M. Kidd, Ph.D., "Glutathione: Systemic Protectant Against Oxidative and Free Radical Damage," *Alternative Medicine Review* 2, no. 3 (1997): 155–176.

10. Jeffrey D. Peterson et al., "Glutathione Levels in Antigen-Presenting Cells Modulate Th1 Versus Th2 Response Patterns," *Proceedings of the National Academy of Sciences USA* 95, no. 6 (March 17, 1998): 3071–3076.

CHAPTER 6

1. John Neustadt and Steve R. Pieczenik, "Medication-Induced Mitochondrial Damage and Disease," *Molecular Nutrition & Food Research* 52, no. 7 (July 2008): 780.

2. Reiner J. Klement and Ulrike Kämmerer, "Is There a Role for Carbohydrate Restriction in the Treatment and Prevention of Cancer?" *Nutrition & Metabolism* 8, no. 75 (October 2011): http://www.nutritionandmetabolism.com/content/pdf/1743-7075-8-75.pdf.

3. George F. Cahill and Richard L. Veech, "Ketoacids? Good medicine?" *Transactions of the American Clinical and Climatological Association* 114 (2003): 149–163.

CHAPTER 7

1. Jill Bolte Taylor, Ph.D., *My Stroke of Insight: A Brain Scientist's Personal Journey* (New York: Viking Penguin, 2008), 146.

2. Douglas Dean and John Mihalasky, *Executive ESP* (Englewood Cliffs: Prentice Hall, 1974).

3. Daniel Kahneman, *Thinking, Fast and Slow* (New York: Farrar, Straus and Giroux, 2011), 11.

4. "Gun Homicides and Gun Ownership by Country," graphic for *The Washington Post*, December 17, 2012: http://www.washingtonpost.com/wp-srv/special/nation/gun-homicides-ownership/table/.

5. Peter Gray, Ph.D., "The Decline of Play and Rise in Children's Mental Disorders," *Psychology Today*, January 26, 2010: http://www.psychologytoday.

com/blog/freedom-learn/201001/the-decline-play-and-rise-in-childrens-mental-disorders; "Any Mental Illness (AMI) among Adults," National Institute of Mental Health: http://www.nimh.nih.gov/statistics/1ANYDIS_adult.shtml; "Major Depression among Adults," National Institute of Mental Health: http://www.nimh.nih.gov/health/statistics/prevalence/major-depression-among-adults.shtml; "Any Anxiety Disorder among Adults," National Institute of Mental Health: http://www.nimh.nih.gov/health/statistics/prevalence/any-anxiety-disorder-among-adults.shtml.

6. Jean M. Twenge et al., "Birth Cohort Increases in Psychopathology among Young Americans, 1938–2007: A Cross-Temporal Meta-analysis of the MMPI," *Clinical Psychology Review* 30, no. 2 (March 2010): 152.

7. William J. Broad, "Seeker, Doer, Giver, Ponderer," *The New York Times*, July 7, 2014, D1.

CHAPTER 8

1. Carl Jung, "The Concept of the Collective Unconscious," in *The Portable Jung*, ed. Joseph Campbell (New York: Viking Penguin, 1971), 60.

CHAPTER 10

1. Rainer J. Klement and Ulrike Kämmerer, "Is There a Role for Carbohydrate Restriction in the Treatment and Prevention of Cancer?" *Nutrition & Metabolism* 8, no. 75 (October 2011): http://www.nutritionandmetabolism.com/content/pdf/1743-7075-8-75.pdf.

CHAPTER 11

1. Stephen Mitchell, *Bhagavad Gita: A New Translation* (New York: Three Rivers Press, 2000), 95.

2. Ibid., 21.

3. Ibid., 88.

4. Swami Nikhilananda, trans., *The Bhagavad Gita* (New York: Ramakrishna-Vivekananda Center, 1944), 285.

5. Mitchell, *Bhagavad Gita*, 105.

CHAPTER 12

1. *The Essential Rumi*, trans. Coleman Barks with John Moyne (San Francisco: HarperSanFrancisco, 1995), 30.

2. "Nagara Sutta: The City," Sutta Nipata 12:65, trans. Thanissaro Bhikkhu (1997): http://www.accesstoinsight.org/tipitaka/sn/sn12/sn12.065.than.html.

3. Chögyam Trungpa, *The Truth of Suffering and the Path of Liberation*, ed. Judith L. Lief (Boston: Shambhala Publications, 2009), 49.

4. Dalai Lama, "10 Questions for the Dalai Lama," *Time*, June 14, 2010: http://content.time.com/time/magazine/article/0,9171,1993865,00.html.

CHAPTER 13

1. Edwin A. M. Gale, "The Rise of Childhood Type 1 Diabetes in the 20th Century," *Diabetes* 51, no. 12 (December 2002): 3353–3361.

2. Dean Ornish et al., "Changes in Prostate Gene Expression in Men Undergoing an Intensive Nutrition and Lifestyle Intervention," *Proceedings of the National Academy of Sciences USA* 105, no. 24 (June 2008): 8369–8374.

CONCLUSION

1. Joseph Campbell, *The Hero with a Thousand Faces* (Novato: New World Library, 2008), 205.

2. Swami Nikhilananda, trans., *The Bhagavad Gita* (New York: Ramakrishna-Vivekananda Center, 1944), 77–78.

3. "Are Shrinking Brains Making Us Smarter?" *Discovery News*, February 7, 2011: http://news.discovery.com/human/psychology/shrinking-brains-intelligence-110207.htm.

4. Campbell, *Hero with a Thousand Faces*, 142.

ACKNOWLEDGMENTS

I would like to thank David Perlmutter, M.D. for repairing my brain after I thought I had lost my mind. Mark Hyman, M.D. helped me to heal my body and discover an extraordinary level of health after Western medicine had given up on me. My shaman teachers in the high Andes healed my soul, showed me the journey beyond death, and the ways to boundless health. These old medicine men and women taught me the principles of One Spirit Medicine and allowed me to taste Infinity.

Patricia Gift at Hay House has been the best ally and support an author could have, and my editors Sally Mason and Joan Oliver were a godsend.

And above all, my deepest gratitude to my wife Marcela Lobos, medicine woman extraordinaire, who healed my heart and patiently loved me while I completed this book.

ABOUT THE AUTHOR

Alberto Villoldo PhD has trained as a psychologist and medical anthropologist, and has studied the healing practices of the Amazon and the Andean shamans for more than 25 years. While an adjunct professor at San Francisco State University, he founded the Biological Self-Regulation Laboratory to study how the brain creates psychosomatic health and disease. Convinced that the mind could create health, he left his laboratory and travelled to the Amazon to work with the medicine men and women of the rainforest and learn their healing methods and mythologies.

Alberto Villoldo directs The Four Winds Society, where he trains individuals in the US and Europe in the practice of shamanic energy medicine. He is the founder of the Light Body School, which has campuses in New York, California, Miami and Germany. He also directs the Center for Energy Medicine in Chile, where he investigates and practices the neuroscience of enlightenment. Alberto Villoldo has written numerous bestselling books, including *Shaman, Healer, Sage; The Four Insights; Courageous Dreaming* and *Power Up Your Brain.*

www.thefourwinds.com

NOTES

NOTES

NOTES

HAY HOUSE TITLES OF RELATED INTEREST

YOU CAN HEAL YOUR LIFE, the movie, starring Louise Hay & Friends
(available as a 1-DVD programme and an expanded 2-DVD set)
Watch the trailer at: www.LouiseHayMovie.com

THE SHIFT, the movie,
starring Dr Wayne W. Dyer
(available as a 1-DVD programme and an expanded 2-DVD set)
Watch the trailer at: www.DyerMovie.com

◙

ALL IS WELL: Heal Your Body with Medicine, Affirmations and Intuition by
Louise Hay and Dr Mona Lisa Schulz

DEFY GRAVITY: Healing Beyond the Bounds of Reason by Caroline Myss

MIND OVER MEDICINE: Scientific Proof that You Can Heal Yourself
by Dr Lissa Rankin

POWER UP YOUR BRAIN: The Neuroscience of Enlightenment,
by Dr David Perlmutter and Alberto Villoldo PhD

All of the above are available at your local bookstore,
or may be ordered by contacting Hay House (see next page).

◙